Praise for *Fanocracy*

"The single most important force in my business is the relationship that I have with my fans. Yes, singing ability, songs, and industry support help tremendously, but the direct fan-to-artist friendship is the most coveted tool in the equation. *Fanocracy* truly emphasizes the importance and how-tos that are necessary to maximize that all-important friendship. I just read it, it's FANTASTIC."

—Ronnie Dunn of Brooks & Dunn

"A focus on the customer is THE essential component for scaling up to build an industry-dominating organization. In *Fanocracy*, David and Reiko offer surprising insights into how to put the needs of people ahead of all else, so that your customers become passionate fans of all you do."

—Verne Harnish, founder of Entrepreneurs' Organization and author of *Scaling Up*

"David and Reiko make the idea of fan culture real, accessible, and actionable for all business—big, small, nonprofit, for-profit, B2B . . . and, yes, even yours! Most of all, they shine a light on the joy of growing a business when you're surrounded by customers who positively LOVE what you do."

—Ann Handley, author of *Everybody Writes* and *Content Rules*

"The most wonderful aspect of David and Reiko's book is how wide-ranging the examples are; nobody can claim fanocracy does not apply to their line of work. And let me tell you, not only is it the most successful way I've ever set up a company, it's also the most fun.

—Gerard Vroomen, cofounder of OPEN Cycle and Cervélo Cycles

FANOCRACY

Also by David Meerman Scott

The New Rules of Marketing & PR
The New Rules of Sales and Service
Marketing the Moon (with Richard Jurek)
Real-Time Marketing & PR
Marketing Lessons from the Grateful Dead (with Brian Halligan)
Newsjacking
World Wide Rave
Tuned In (with Craig Stull and Phil Myers)
Cashing In with Content
Eyeball Wars

Also by Reiko Scott

"Phantom Limb"

Turning Fans
into Customers

FANOCRACY

and Customers
into Fans

David Meerman Scott and Reiko Scott

FOREWORD BY TONY ROBBINS

PORTFOLIO / PENGUIN

Portfolio / Penguin
An imprint of Penguin Random House LLC
penguinrandomhouse.com

Most Portfolio books are available at a discount when purchased in quantity for sales
promotions or corporate use. Special editions, which include personalized covers, excerpts, and
corporate imprints, can be created when purchased in large quantities. For more information,
please call (212) 572-2232 or e-mail specialmarkets@penguinrandomhouse.com. Your local
bookstore can also assist with discounted bulk purchases using the
Penguin Random House corporate Business-to-Business program. For assistance
in locating a participating retailer, e-mail B2B@penguinrandomhouse.com.

Library of Congress Cataloging-in-Publication Data

ISBN 9780593084007 (hardcover)
ISBN 9780593084014 (ebook)

Printed in Canada
1   3   5   7   9   10   8   6   4   2

BOOK DESIGN BY LUCIA BERNARD

Penguin is committed to publishing works of quality and integrity.
In that spirit, we are proud to offer this book to our readers; however, the story,
the experiences, and the words are the author's alone.

MAR 1 3 2020

CONTENTS

HeadCount: Musicians for Democracy
The Secret Language of Passionate People

CHAPTER 14: SHARE YOUR FANDOM

FOREWORD

Tony Robbins

———————

The core strategy behind any remarkable organization—one that dwarfs the competition and creates massive customer loyalty—is to provide *so much value* that customers can't help but share their enthusiasm and excitement. This is what I call "Creating Raving Fan Customers" and is one of the 7 Forces that I teach at my Business Mastery seminars around the world.

Those whom David and Reiko term "fandom" customers are loyal. They know who you really are, and they stick around even when you move in new directions because you've added value to them in a way that nobody else can.

Customers who are merely satisfied can leave you. You and everyone on your team must be obsessed with doing whatever it takes to create a fanocracy in your organization. You need to create a culture in which your *entire reason for being* is to make sure that your clients are continuously blown away.

This obsession with adding more value—doing more for your clients than anyone else on earth—has been the secret sauce for the thirty-three companies that I have the privilege to own and help grow. We now have over twelve hundred employees with combined revenues of over $5 billion, and together our teams have grown because, for us, customer *satisfaction* is not enough! We don't make the mistake of falling in love with our products and services—we fall more in love with our clients.

And it all starts with you. When you live an extraordinary life and have a mission of serving a purpose higher than yourself, you radiate energy and passion that draws others to you—whether it's customers, business partners, or employees.

Every single person in your entire business culture is part of a team of enthusiasts who have the power to create more enthusiasts. If you are a company of two people, then both of you get to build the culture, your "fandom." If you are an army of ten thousand or one hundred thousand, then each of you plays a part in building the culture. *You empower and motivate your team to take the initiative and make the tough decisions that inspire lifetime loyalty, and when you do, you create fanocracy.*

Any organization can succeed by implementing the ideas in *Fanocracy.* And by reading it, you are taking the steps necessary to differentiate your business by cultivating fandom.

David Meerman Scott is a dear friend and I've followed his ideas for years. More than a decade ago, he was among the very first people to identify the social media revolution as it was beginning. Now he is the lead marketing speaker at my Business Mastery seminars, and audiences from around the world love his informative, entertaining, and inspiring talks. No one knows more about new ways to reach buyers. He's introduced strategies to the Business Mastery community, like newsjacking, that reinvent the way entrepreneurs engage the marketplace and grow business.

In *Fanocracy*, David and Reiko are together breaking new ground. *Fanocracy* is a deep dive into the strategies to build a powerful culture that drives business success. *Fanocracy* also explores the thinking of a new generation—one that values community and sharing. David and Reiko share surprising ideas you can implement immediately, such as letting go of your work and allowing people to make it their own, seeing the world as a gift and giving gifts in return, and celebrating your customers' stories.

PART I

What's a Fanocracy
and Why Do You
Need One?

CHAPTER 1

Our Story

by David & Reiko

David:

It was September 2007 and I'd been invited to meet the management team of an early stage marketing software startup in their office in Cambridge, Massachusetts. They informed me in their invitation email that their entire company of ten people read my newly published book *The New Rules of Marketing & PR*.

How could I not look forward to meeting them after an email like that?

They said their company was developing software to help small and medium-sized businesses take advantage of the trends and techniques I described in my book.

"We've been eager to meet you, David," welcomed Brian, the cofounder and CEO, as we entered the cramped conference room in the company's shared office space. "The concepts in your book are exactly what we've built our company on. It's uncanny how similar our perspectives are."

In those days, nearly every marketer on the planet spent buckets of money on traditional advertising and hired salespeople to cold-call prospects. My *New Rules of Marketing & PR* introduced a new perspective to the future of marketing. It described the enormous and far-reaching power I saw with social media. That was back in the days when MySpace was more popular than Facebook, and Snapchat and Instagram didn't yet exist. It was a thrilling experience to be with people starting a company to help other businesses implement the ideas I wrote about in my book.

I eased into a chair at a table across from Brian and several of his colleagues.

"How did you come up with the idea for your company?" I asked.

Brian replied, "We were classmates at MIT Sloan's MBA program and always talked about how the way people buy products and services has changed so dramatically. Google is the first place people go, so, as you said in your book, web content is more important than advertising. We decided that after we graduated, we'd form a startup to develop software that helps companies get found in the search engines. It's what we call inbound marketing."

"Great timing to launch the company," I said as I removed my MacBook Pro from my backpack and opened it. "There's no question that people are beginning to realize the importance—"

"Hang on," Brian said, pointing at my laptop. "This meeting can't go any further until you tell me about those *stickers*!"

I showcase my passions to the world by personalizing the stark aluminum of my Apple notebook.

My computer is a billboard of what I love.

"What's with the Japan sticker?" asked Brian.

The Japanese script is not something most people recognize, and I was surprised he had placed it immediately.

"Japan is really important to me," I said. "I was an exchange student for a summer in high school, I lived in Japan for seven years from 1987 to 1993, and my wife, Yukari, is Japanese."

Brian looked surprised. "Are you serious? I lived in Japan for a few years in the 1990s too." His finger moved to another sticker among the many spread across my computer.

"What's the deal with the Nantucket one?"

My Nantucket sticker was rather subtle, a silhouette map of the island. If Brian could identify it, he must have visited and knew the island.

"I've got a house on the island. Have you been?" I asked, although I suspected I already knew the answer.

Brian nodded. "Have been going for years. This is weird. It's like we're long-lost brothers. We both go to Nantucket, we both lived in Japan, and we both saw the future of marketing early on."

He paused for a moment and then grinned. "And a Stealie! So you're a Deadhead too?"

Brian was right.

This is *getting really weird*, I silently agreed. If he knew what a Stealie was, then Brian was big into the Grateful Dead too. Many people recognize the half-red, half-blue skull symbol first used as a cover illustration on the band's 1976 album *Steal Your Face*, yet only true fans use the word "Stealie" to describe it.

"Absolutely! I've been to dozens of shows. They're my favorite band."

"They're my favorite too," Brian added. "I've been to over *fifty* shows!"

By then, I realized that Brian's colleagues were intently following our animated conversation. They seemed genuinely happy to let us geek out about the Grateful Dead.

"You going to the Phil Lesh show at the Orpheum in a few weeks?" I asked Brian.

Lesh was the Grateful Dead's founding bassist. Since Jerry Garcia's death in 1995 and the breakup of the band, the original members frequently tour with their own bands and in various combinations.

"I'm going for sure but haven't finalized my plans."

Right away I understood Brian's Deadhead code. He wanted to go but didn't have a ticket yet.

"I've got a spare ticket, want to join me?"

In a matter of minutes, Brian and I went from being complete strangers to talking like old friends because of the instant bond triggered by stickers on my computer.

After that first Phil Lesh concert in October 2007, we attended some fifty more shows together. Brian and I even combined our Grateful Dead fandom and our shared passion for marketing when we co-wrote the book *Marketing Lessons from the Grateful Dead: What Every Business Can Learn from the Most Iconic Band in History*. Interestingly, the Japanese language edition of the book became the fourth most popular business book in Japan the year it was published, outselling the English language version that year. Were Brian and I unconsciously channeling our experiences in Japan when writing? Who knows?

A few days after our initial meeting, Brian invited me to become the founding member of the HubSpot advisory board. It was a thrill to add a HubSpot sticker to my computer to mark the occasion. Over the years, I worked closely with Brian and the HubSpot team to help grow the business to a projected $650 million in revenue in 2019. The company is now publicly traded on the New York Stock Exchange and has offices around the world. When HubSpot opened a Japan office in 2016, Brian and I both delivered presentations at the opening event.

All of this happened because Brian and I found a common

language, common interests, common fandom. We shared our passions with each other, first for the music we both loved, and then for our work.

Reiko:

For days I had been nervous to meet with Dr. Azra Raza, the director of the Myelodysplastic Syndrome Center at Columbia University Medical Center in New York City, who was to be my new adviser. In 2013, I had just finished my second year at Columbia and had dreams of being a doctor, and this summer lab position would be another stepping-stone to that goal. That's exactly how I thought about it—merely another box to check on a future application or a résumé. I prepared myself for the kind of dismissive greetings I had experienced in previous lab environments. Because of my past research experiences, as I entered her office, I stepped into the academic persona I'd cultured to fit the cold and sterile rooms I'd become accustomed to, just as an actress would, auditioning for the role of a laboratory scientist.

Instead, I was welcomed by a woman in an intimate library filled with shelves and shelves of books. Not only medical journals but history books, autobiographies, and novels. I felt as if I had traveled back in time to the home where I grew up, where books overflowed from the high shelves and were stacked on the floors because there was never enough room for all of them. I grew up with parents who passed their profound love of books on to me. As my eyes grazed the titles, my fingers itched to flip through them. I was so dazzled that I didn't think to introduce myself.

My new adviser caught me staring, captivated.

"Do you like poetry?" she asked.

I didn't know what to say. In my two years of undergraduate lab work, I never began a conversation like this. Science and art were two separate things, not made to mix, right? That, at the time, was what I'd believed, so I continually and unconsciously silenced the part of me that wanted both.

"Yes," I answered softly.

From previous interviews I learned not to out myself as being too enthusiastic, as I assumed my love of stories and words was a weakness, one a scientist would not relate to.

Dr. Raza picked up a book from her desk and read to me in a language I didn't understand. Then she followed with the English translation recited from memory. The words flowed musically as she looked back to me. "I love this one," she said. "I've been working on the translation."

"It's beautiful," I said.

She smiled and gestured for me to sit. Although we had just met, we began talking about books and science. I felt as if I'd stepped back into a comfortable conversation we'd had many times before.

I felt as though I never wanted to leave.

Over the two summers I spent in Dr. Raza's lab, I observed how her unbridled passion for literature—her self-professed obsession—made her a better doctor. Passion, I realized, wasn't a distraction, it was a way of connecting people on a deeper level. Just as it had connected us.

Her enthusiasm for translation from Arabic and Urdu to English wound its way to the translation of her patients' ills. She gushed to her longtime patients about the Hannah Arendt movie that she had seen last week and, in turn, encouraged her patients to talk about that which gave them the most pleasure. She was curious about them. What made them feel good? What brought them joy? There seemed to be no end to the interest she had in each of her patients.

"You can't work with anyone if you don't know who they are and what they love," she said. "We treat the person, not the illness."

Eventually, I learned that this kind of practice had a name: narrative medicine.

Dr. Raza helped me to nurture similar passions. I learned what was, to me, a profound lesson, how art could touch science.

It took a mentor who shared my interests—who encouraged me to lean in to the activities I loved instead of dismissing them as mere hobbies—to change how I saw myself. Learning how to incorporate all of who I am into my professional life made me not only a better health-care provider but also a happier person. That has been the greatest and most lasting gift of our time together.

After I left Dr. Raza's lab and graduated from Columbia in 2015, I carried those lessons with me to Boston University School of Medicine (BUSM). As a second-year medical student, I created a syllabus and taught a class on narrative medicine at BUSM. I found my way forward because of the new way I labeled myself by modeling the way Dr. Raza labeled herself.

I saw my experience as a complement to my father's collaboration with Brian Halligan. I saw how shared passions build lasting bridges that lead to professional success. These passions can be fostered in communities that persist long after as each individual continues on their professional path forward.

Being a fan builds close connections to others with whom we share interests. The behavior and its results can be a model for others to mirror.

———

The two of us, father and daughter, are obviously different; however, our observations on the state of the world today are uncannily similar.

As we discussed our experiences over the past few years, we were surprised at how important our passions and the fandom worlds we inhabit are to our lives. The father loves surfing because being out on the water and interacting with other surfers helps him relax and clear his mind. The daughter loves to draw and share fan art of the books she loves for the same reason. And, over time, we both realized how alike our views are on growing a business by tapping into fandom.

Because of the changing nature of the world, it's essential to understand how to reach all kinds of people, including millennials and Generation Z as well as those of all races and orientations. It is for this reason that we've researched and written together.

In the chapters that follow, we take deep dives into major elements of developing fans, including the importance of proximity to customers, letting go of your work, giving gifts without any expectation of something in return, harnessing the power of transparency in business, and other concepts. Through interviews, examples of success, and a set of strategies, we looked at how entities of all kinds—including companies large and small, nonprofits, entrepreneurs, restaurants, artists, musicians, teachers, health-care professionals, and insurance agents—can tap into fan cultures and connect deeply with followers.

As we discussed our experiences over many nights across the dinner table, we began to consider the ideas that you will now find in our book. It was a sharp reminder to both of us that hobbies and passions don't disappear as soon as one steps into "adult" or "professional" life. We both agree that the myth of unyielding professionalism can obscure our genuine connections. That's why we chose to write this book.

Exchanging texts about television shows or comic books has gotten daughter, Reiko, through study hours that extended far into nights that would have otherwise felt endless. And father, David, has forged deep, lifelong friendships with those who are as passionate about live music as he is.

To love things outside work is to make meaningful connections with like-minded people.

To achieve the success that comes with developing passionate fans of your business, fandom culture is necessary. Yet there's another important reason to understand these ideas, as we said earlier: exposing ourselves to people who share our interests leads us to live happier lives. And when you can introduce your fandom passions and bring in others who are completely different from you and *they* become fans, you create an ideal environment—a place where great things happen.

An understanding of how and why people become passionate about a company, product, idea, or artist serves as a way to do business. This understanding also delivers a blueprint to bring friends and family together to celebrate what they love, a place everyone wants to be part of because they can be their authentic selves and successful at the same time.

CHAPTER 2

Strength Through Fandom

by Reiko

On the afternoon of April 15, 2013, Patriots' Day, the crowds were dense at Copley Square near the finish line of the Boston Marathon as people cheered on their friends and loved ones, or simply enjoyed the spectacle. That day, I was a few hundred miles away at college in New York City, but I had grown up around Boston and still thought of it as home. Patriots' Day had always been one of my favorite days of the year, perhaps because it was so Boston in nature—few people outside Massachusetts knew that we had a legal holiday on the anniversary of the first battle of the American Revolution. The whole state shuts down so people can participate in or watch Revolutionary War reenactments, parades, and the Boston Marathon. Patriots' Day reminded me of early mornings in my hometown, drinking coffee while getting into my marching band uniform, preparing for the celebration. Away at school, that day I felt especially nostalgic.

The festive air of celebration of that afternoon was shattered in an instant when two homemade pressure cooker bombs detonated, killing 3 and injuring more than 250 people.

My cell phone buzzed with activity and Patriots' Day was on everyone's tongue and keyboard. I gathered scattered news stories of a bombing . . . unknown suspects . . . police activity . . . casualties . . . screams, sirens, and mass confusion. I knew that several of my friends were running the marathon that day, and even more were attending as spectators. I scrolled through Facebook for updates that popped up sporadically from people I knew. "Safe. Crossed the finish line at 2:30 and on my way home," one friend's status update read. "Was watching from Comm Ave, not near danger," another reported.

As I learned that the people I cared about were uninjured, I grew calmer, but there was a lingering uneasiness in me that I couldn't shake. My sense of detached reassurance, being so far from home, was disquieting. Digital proximity wasn't enough. No amount of news from the manhunt or police spokesperson's pronouncements could touch the emotional heart of my unease, and the echoing fear and confusion that bounced around social media added to that discomfort. What I needed was to be near other Bostonians after this tragedy, to reach out and feel those human connections, and remind myself that those stayed strong.

The Boston Red Sox: Uniting the City of Boston

Ask any Boston native about what it means to be from our city, and the majority will say we are the best sports city in the world. Since the year 2000, Boston sports teams have collectively won twelve championships: six in American football by the Patriots, four in baseball by the Red Sox, one in basketball by the Celtics, and one in hockey by the Bruins. With a record like that, it isn't easy to refute the claim. However, the record alone isn't what makes sports in this city so important, it's how tied it is to Boston's cultural identity.

After the bombing, the manhunt spread to the suburbs, the news was alive with the words "terrorism" and "suspects" and "lockdown" and "firefight," and I was looking for something to cling to that would unite us as a city, rather than going through the aftermath of this tragedy alone. Miraculously, out of that chaos came something that united me and other Bostonians watching from afar on our phones or TVs. That most stable, unifying factor turned out to be something that might surprise you.

On Friday, April 19, the Boston Red Sox were required to cancel their home game against the Kansas City Royals because the city was still on lockdown, allowing authorities to search for the remaining suspect, who was finally apprehended that evening after four days on the run.

With the arrest of the second of the two men charged with the bombing, the city was finally cleared to return to "normal" activities. But it didn't yet feel normal. The hashtag #BostonStrong was already spreading around social media, yet people needed more than that. They needed faces to put to Boston Strong. They needed to be around like-minded people in a crowd, cheering with others at their side for a city they loved.

Soon after, less than a week following an attack on a huge sporting event in Boston, the Red Sox were slated to play their first game at Fenway Park since the tragedy. Tens of thousands of spectators gathered in the most recognizable baseball park in the country, and millions watched on television. The Red Sox organization realized this particular game was the opportunity to unite our city.

Before a cheering crowd of over thirty-five thousand at Fenway, Boston Red Sox star player David Ortiz, affectionately referred to as "Big Papi" by Red Sox Nation, took the mic:

All right, all right, Boston.
This jersey that we wear today.

It doesn't say Red Sox. It says Boston.

We want to thank you, Mayor Menino, Governor Patrick, and
* the whole police department for the great job that they did this*
* past week.*

This is our fucking city, and nobody gonna dictate our freedom!

Stay strong. Thank you!

Something irrevocably changed after that short speech, after that game. The Red Sox became more than a sports team as the people of Boston united behind them. While some might think a baseball game is nothing more than a frivolous distraction at an important time, it proved to be much more to a grieving city, serving as a catalyst to move beyond the bombing. From 2013 to 2016, Boston's economic growth rates surpassed the US national average, with gross city product estimated at $119.1 billion in 2016 according to *Boston's Economy 2018*, published by the Boston Planning & Development Agency Research Division. Unemployment has also been steadily dropping, from 7 percent in 2013 down to a rate of 3.1 percent in 2017, with total jobs increasing faster within the city than the national average.

Being a fan of a baseball team became synonymous with being proud of your city. It was a rallying cry that echoed in the years that followed.

The Red Sox rode the energy of Boston Strong all the way to the World Series, where they defeated the St. Louis Cardinals in six games, bringing home another championship for the most decorated city in recent sports history. By then, it wasn't about bragging rights or statistics anymore. Sports fandom had transformed the resiliency of a city affected by a terrible event, and the triumphs embodied the emotions of the entire Boston community.

What or Who Is a Fan?

What was the secret ingredient that the Red Sox were able to tap into during the fear and confusion in those days after the bombing? What did they have that news outlets or government officials didn't?

They had fans.

The Red Sox were able to channel the shared meaning of their fandom into something more, cutting through the chaos of those dark days.

A fan?

The stereotype often portrayed of a sports superfan isn't usually an attractive one: a guy in his midforties, with a growing beer belly, spilling chips on his sofa and cursing at the TV with a voice so loud it deafens the neighbors.

Or another stereotypical fan we've become familiar with: the socially awkward thirtysomething nerd, living in his parents' basement, playing video games like *Call of Duty* or *World of Warcraft*. If he's feeling old-school, he'll whip out some dice for Dungeons & Dragons. What are his chances of finding a significant other?

Or how about another popular version: a teenage girl so goo-goo eyed over a celebrity that she's covered her walls with his face and changed her usernames on every social media site to something like HotBoyLovr05. She runs a blog devoted to stalking the whereabouts of the celebrity and reads vampire romance novels. Her squeals of excitement startle everyone in a ten-foot vicinity. Can we count on her to contribute meaningfully to society?

We can be conditioned to view some people as stereotypes of fandom, such as the socially awkward characters depicted on television shows like *The Big Bang Theory* or *Revenge of the Nerds*. Many assume fandom is only for those holed up in their basements or starry-eyed teenage girls or the *otaku*.

Are these extremes the only ways to be a fan? Is it true that those who commit their time and effort to what others might consider frivolous hobbies are living less meaningful lives than people who single-mindedly pursue their education and careers?

We have come to the conclusion that too many people limit their own enjoyment of the things they love. Do they worry that pouring their hearts into the activities they enjoy might affect how others see them? Are they afraid of being reduced to a mere stereotype?

We all have interests that engage us, and we use these to reach out to others, whether it be a short "Did you watch the game last night?" during your lunch break or an invitation to watch the new Marvel movie release in theaters next weekend. Interests connect us. Fandoms connect us. That's the kind of human connection we crave.

The Lonely Chaos of the Digital Age

The internet brings promise of tremendous easy engagement with audiences around the world. Social networks such as Facebook and content distribution services like YouTube are free and simple to use, and reach every human on the planet with an internet connection, so it's no wonder that billions of people around the world have gravitated toward them.

In the earliest days of social media, participating in these networks was like a virtual cocktail party. We could meet with our friends and ask what they were up to. We could stay in touch after school or work.

We've posted, shared, liked, and upvoted, and it was an enjoyable and effective way to stay in touch or reconnect with people we haven't seen in a long while.

But today, it's another story altogether. The algorithms deployed by social networks like Facebook don't show us what we want to see, because the technology favors profit for shareholders rather than the original promise of allowing people to interact with their friends, families, and colleagues. We get tidal waves of spam email and social networks that display advertisements instead of messages from our friends, and fake news instead of what we, as humans, really need to know to lead fulfilling and productive lives.

Worse, scammers have figured out how to game the networks to lure people into partisan content loops to prey on our worst fears and create new ones. While most people understand that a free social network means some loss of privacy, we didn't sign up to have our innermost thoughts, secrets, and notes to ourselves and loved ones stolen and sold to the highest bidder.

The result is a polarizing and cold digital world. Many people now feel that the promise of online social connection just isn't for them anymore—the romance is over. Many people have told us that they have canceled their online presence and opted for privacy they can control themselves.

We found the following information interesting: in yearly surveys of over one million eighth, tenth, and twelfth graders in the United States, those who use more electronic communications are *less happy*, according to a 2018 report by Jean M. Twenge, Gabrielle N. Martin, and W. Keith Campbell. Their research shows that psychological well-being (measured by self-esteem, life satisfaction, and happiness) suddenly decreased after 2012, when smartphone usage shot up. And it's not just adolescent users of electronic communications who are unhappy. We all feel the increasing stress related to keeping up appearances online.

The pendulum has swung too far in the direction of superficial online communications at a time when people are hungry for true human connection.

Our book was born from our growing frustration with digital gimmickery. There's something broken and we all feel it. *We are on the cusp of an important cultural shift.*

We've seen similar important cultural shifts in the past.

For example, starting in the 1950s, Americans became excited about the promise of processed foods. Swanson TV dinners, Pringles Newfangled Potato Chips, and Stove Top stuffing became the rage. Fast-food restaurants such as McDonald's exploded in popularity. The media gushed about how increased shelf life and ease of preparation would make everyone's lives easier.

But America has swung back in a big way in recent years as people have begun to realize that processed food isn't good for our health. And it doesn't taste so great either! Many Americans now think differently about food. We shop and cook in ways that would be more familiar to our great-grandparents. We crave fresh vegetables, happily go out of our way to shop at farmers' markets, and pay extra for free-range chicken.

We see the same shift playing out in the world of human communications. We've gone too far into manufactured friendship through social media, and something different is coming next. *The pendulum is swinging back to genuine, authentic human connections.*

Online presence brought me and others little comfort when the city of Boston was in crisis. What did help us was the united force of a community of people rallying together behind a passion for a winning sports team.

Too many organizations react to digital chaos by doubling down, trying to shout ever louder, outdoing one another about their products and services in social media and other online channels. Uninvited, they send us their email blasts hyping their offerings with increasing frequency. They try to get through to us, past all of the noise, by creating and sending *more* videos, *more* tweets, and requesting *more* LinkedIn connections. It's become too easy to spray content out via social media without a long-term strategy. After all, it takes just a minute or two to write and send a tweet.

The solution isn't to do more of the same. It takes more heart to start a movement.

In a digital world where our lives are increasingly cluttered and superficial, we're missing something tremendously powerful: *genuine human connection*. People are going to be most invested in that which creates a sense of intimacy, warmth, and shared meaning in a world that would otherwise relegate them to a statistic.

The solution to any frustration about the lack of human connection in our lives is easy. It's up to us to develop and nurture what we are most passionate about. For me and my father, it's going to concerts or book clubs with friends or cosplaying at Comic Con. For others, it might be running, playing golf, doing needlepoint, going to plays, collecting fine wine, spending Saturday afternoons at art galleries and museums, taking writing classes, going to conferences, practicing yoga, hitting the gym, gardening, or fishing.

Fandom is everywhere. It's the key for any organization, artist, solopreneur, or other entity to be successful in bringing people to-gether. Fandom spans generations and subject matter to bind individu-als together in excitement, purpose, and buying power. No matter whom you're dealing with, understanding fandom is the cornerstone to your success.

We call this act of consciously bringing people together through a shared endeavor a *fanocracy*: an organization or person that honors fans and consciously fosters meaningful connections among them.

The suffix "-cracy," from the Greek *kratos* for "rule," is used in pop-ular culture as well as in academia to mean government by a particular sort of people or according to a particular principle. A fanocracy is a culture where fans rule, and that's what we see emerging in today's world. We are moving into an era that prizes people over products.

When we build on our individual strengths to achieve greatness together, fanocracy comes alive.

The fundamental ingredient for true fandom—meaningful and ac-tive human connection—demonstrates a shift in the way a company re-lates to its customers. It is more forthright, helpful, and transparent. It creates new experiences by turning customers into like-minded, en-thusiastic fans. After all, it was fanocracy that drew Boston together to cheer the Red Sox to victory.

A true fanocracy mobilizes people to think, feel, and act together with a helpful, positive force during difficult times. In the medical world I'm in, it means a healing force in the healthy exchange between patients and doctors. Fanocracy empowers people in a way that no

single individual would ever be able to accomplish by himself or herself. *Mastering life happens when the joy we have in our work and play
feels the same.*

**Building connections to like-minded people leads
to success in our business and joy in our heart.**

This Is My City

Despite growing up in Boston, the city of champions, when I was
younger, I didn't follow professional sports. My friends wore team jer-
seys to school, or I'd hear them talk excitedly about the names of players. In those days my passions were focused elsewhere, so their
discussions didn't affect me. Even later, after we graduated from college, I was uninterested in participating in conversations about sports
with my now husband, Ben, who, as long as I've known him, has been
a die-hard baseball fan. He religiously reads the sports news for updates on the Yankees' lineup. I had, I now realize, a perhaps arrogant or
dismissive assumption that being a fan of a sports team was frivolous.
After all, didn't it waste a lot of time? And what would you possibly do
with all that sports data?

Later, when I moved back to Boston for medical school, I found
myself more interested in the sports culture so ingrained into our city.
I started to see that it was *more than just a game* to many people around
me; it was a *culture*. Even now, at Boston Medical Center, the same
hospital where many of the Boston Marathon bombing victims were
first sent, and the hospital where I now work and study, our staff often
wear "Team BMC" shirts in the styles of the Red Sox or Celtics logos.

In bars around the city, there are framed photos of David Ortiz, accompanied by his now famous speech. That's fanocracy in action.

And, surprising to everyone around me (most of all to myself), I grew very attached to one sport in particular: hockey. I became a Boston Bruins fan, having never watched a hockey game, on TV or in person, until my midtwenties. I learned what the rules are—what is a penalty and what is a good old-fashioned "check." I got to know the players' names and stats and felt, finally—through my immersion—that I was a part of this city of champions. I went to my first game and was on my feet with the thousands of others at TD Garden when the Bruins scored in overtime.

It gave me a side effect I didn't anticipate. It allowed me a common language with my father-in-law, with whom I had never shared similar interests or had much to become excited about. Yet here we suddenly were, two Bruins fans. We could talk about the last game and what we thought would happen next. He gave me a Bruins sweatshirt for my birthday, which I wore proudly to the next game. We'll both be cheering on the team we love to the Stanley Cup this season.

A fandom doesn't always have to unite a whole city. Sometimes it's enough just to unite two people.

Cue the duck boats.

CHAPTER 3

The Power of Fan-Centric Business

by David

was on hold, again, with yet another representative from a web hosting and domain registration company. This was now the sixth person I had spoken with in less than a week. I also emailed a dozen requests, getting a few replies but from a different person each time and no resolution to my problem with their responses. The problem with one of my internet domains was apparently so unusual that each person I spoke with hadn't encountered the problem before and didn't know how to fix it. I was bounced from one department to the next, one support level to another, with no end in sight.

Two years before, when I first became a client of the hosting company, the representative set up my account incorrectly. He checked a box indicating a particular service type that after two years, upon renewal, would erase all the data in my account, including years of email history, unless changed before renewal. But nobody knew how to make the change. (I know, I couldn't believe it either!) It wasn't something anyone would take lightly, and with the second anniversary fast approaching, I was determined to avoid the looming disaster. No one had an immediate solution to the digital catastrophe I was facing.

Each rep had been friendly enough and seemed eager to help, but each time I had to explain my problem from the beginning, and it was taking ten to twenty minutes to detail what the other reps had already learned, what had been tried previously, and what I thought might need to happen next. Each time I was placed on "a brief hold" by the representative as they "researched the problem." Eventually, every person I spoke with told me they couldn't immediately solve the problem and would need to "escalate" it. As this unfolded, I became more exasperated because nobody had taken the initiative to own the problem. Nobody offered to follow up, ensuring that someone knowledgeable would correct the problem. I was on my own. It was frustrating, to say the least.

Why didn't this company assign one person to take charge of my problem and see it through to the conclusion? That would not only help me but also save hours of effort by the multiple reps who tried to help me. Why was this company willing to lose resources on so much wasted effort?

With dozens of web hosting and domain registration companies competing for my business, why didn't this one see any value in developing a long-term relationship with me rather than just selling one product to me? Heck, as it is, I own over two dozen internet domains and spend thousands of dollars a year on services. You might say I'm a reliable, qualified, and desired customer. Wouldn't you think they'd want to keep my business for the foreseeable years to come?

Go Beyond the Product

For the past fifty years, business has followed a predictable blueprint as taught by business schools around the world: companies build products and services that appeal to large numbers of people and market them to consumers by advertising through mainstream media, including television, radio, newspapers, magazines, and direct mail. In this model, customer service is a cost to be controlled by spending as little possible. In our past world, where we all read the same newspapers, watched the same television shows, shopped at the same local stores, and brushed our teeth with similar toothpastes, this model seemed to work. Merely facilitating the sale of products and services was an adequate way to fulfill a company's role.

Today, because of the rise of the web and the ability to see exactly the information we want, when we want, consumers have changed how we research products and services and how we buy them. We have near perfect information and can buy online from suppliers across the globe in seconds. We can read the comments on the products or service from other consumers. *Competition has a brand-new face today.*

Competition used to be down the street. Now it's everywhere.

In this new digital world, as Reiko mentioned in chapter 2, we're missing the power of genuine human connection, the single most important ingredient for creating a fanocracy. I had no connection with the web hosting company, because I never spoke with the same person twice. I felt as if I were merely customer number 12,286 with a trouble ticket, a problem to pass off. With the string of reps who *tried* to help me, do you think I felt an emotional bond as I was about to lose all my data?

This is such an easy, yet powerful, mind-set shift to be made by an organization! Building a relationship with customers cultivates fandom,

while simply selling products to customers means it is easier for somebody to instantly move on to another brand that's cheaper and more
convenient or that knows how to problem-solve. If I had just one person
who showed initiative with the hosting company, I would have felt I had
a partner at that organization for years to come.

Some people might assume that their business or profession isn't
conducive to building fans. They might say: "I'm a _____, I
can't create a fanocracy." (Fill in the blank with "software company
marketer," "accountant," "doctor," "lawyer," "technology salesperson,"
"artist," "furniture store owner," "insurance salesperson," or whatever
kind of professional you are.) The fact is, every type of business can
create a fanocracy by building personal relationships with their
customers.

> ### The relationships we build with our customers
> ### are more important than the products
> ### and services we sell to them.

In fact, some of the most interesting examples of fanocracy are companies that sell a product or service that's seen as a *commodity* in the
minds of customers. The web hosting services I mentioned at the beginning of this chapter are only one example, because when you think
about it, web hosting is a commodity like insurance or underwear.

In our research, we were thrilled to uncover a wide variety of
successful organizations that have grown their businesses in remarkable ways. These organizations found success that is atypical of their
industries.

MeUndies: The Story of a Subscription Underpants Company

An unlikely company that is developing fans is called MeUndies. Look at the company's online store. Do you like it? I did. So, what the heck, I tried a pair of underpants. The MicroModal fabric was remarkably soft and stretchy and the design was awesome, so I bought a few more. Then I learned about their subscription service. What? *Subscription service?* For *underwear?*

MeUndies is a clever combination of fantastic underwear designs and effective online technology all designed to cultivate fans. Technology for underpants? Yes! The company's subscription platform makes buying new underpants an enjoyable experience. I confess I actually look forward to choosing a new pair each month.

Subscribers initially choose the type, size, and print style—Classic, Bold, or Adventurous (for me it is Adventurous, at sixteen dollars a month—I love the loud, vibrant prints). Then, anytime you want, you can log in to the platform and see eight or ten different print options. A mere click of the mouse reserves your pair, shipped out on the same day each month. What makes this particularly fun is that the prints change on a regular basis. Some are limited editions—if you don't buy now, you're out of luck. Some are exclusive to those who subscribe and can't be bought as a one-off.

As I look at my plan right now, the options are Candy Corn (patterned like the Halloween candy), Lights Out (glow-in-the-dark ghosts), Space Cadet (planets and other space-themed things), Victory Lap (a checkerboard), Penguin Party (black-and-white penguins against a pink background) and several others that are equally interesting. So this month I decided on Penguin Party for my new underwear.

Yukari is sure to be thrilled! She loves penguins. In fact, we went to Antarctica together a few years ago so she could be with penguins where they live.

You can see where I'm going with this: I went from decades of dreading the thought of buying underwear whenever the old ones started to get holes or started falling down to eagerly awaiting options for my next month's subscription delivery.

Other companies are busy creating a never-ending flood of product advertising and social media hype. Ten percent off! Free shipping! Faster, better, newer, cheaper! But because of overwhelming digital clutter, this approach means that these companies are forced to focus on products and services instead of what they should be focusing on—*people*, their living, breathing customers!

"We're creating a brand that's relatable and speaks to the consumer eye to eye," says MeUndies founder and chairman, Jonathan Shokrian. "Our family of customers feel an emotional connection to our brand, something that's historically been missing in our product category."

Social media outlets like Instagram play an instrumental role in the company's sales growth, with @MeUndies on Instagram having 340,000 followers as I write this. A particularly interesting aspect of MeUndies is the ability to buy matching pairs—the same print is available for men and women. That means everyone can sport the same design—couples' pairs or a matching batch as a fun gift for friends. The company's Instagram frequently features couples who are fans of MeUndies showing off their matching pairs.

Many people who work in online businesses tell us they can't build fans because they don't have opportunities to interact with people. However, the unlikely business of selling underwear by online subscription, having subscription-customer-only patterns, offering matching pairs for couples, and providing opportunities for underwear enthusiasts to see and be seen on social networks showing off their favorites are all novel ways to build fans! By offering customers an opportunity to participate in how the brand is presented to the world, they are more likely to become emotionally invested in experiencing it.

"Although we sell underwear, we stand for so much more than the product," Shokrian says. "We're empowering people to live a life of boldness, and what's really important are the values and lifestyle that we stand for."

I agree. I'm now a massive MeUndies fan. And it's because, unlike at the web hosting company, I feel as if the people at MeUndies understand me. I sometimes think they stay awake at night dreaming up new ways to understand me even better! Even their recent tagline is among my very favorite in the world: "9 Million Happy Butts*and Going Strong"!

To be successful in a world where fans rule, we must be convinced that relationships with customers are more important than the products or services we sell to them. Meaningful human connection, the fundamental ingredient for true fandom, can be created by all kinds of different companies, even those who never meet customers in person or speak with them on the telephone.

Hagerty Insurance: It's Not Products and Services, It's People

"Insurance sucks," says McKeel Hagerty, CEO of Hagerty Insurance Agency, a specialty provider of classic-car insurance. "Nobody wants to buy insurance. It's not fun." Rather than just talk up the company's insurance products, like everyone else in the industry does, McKeel came up with a knockout creative idea: build human connections be-tween classic-car owners and his company, which insures them.

"As I started reflecting on the opportunity that we had in front of us, I thought that this isn't about insurance. Instead, it's really about protecting a person's passion for their car," McKeel told us. "I didn't have to invent the car and I didn't have to create the passion, I just have to tap into it and tie together the spirit around it. And that's the core idea for us. It's the mechanism around which we have a much more emotional, relationship-oriented connection with our clients and how we get and keep our fans."

Bond with your customers by taking an interest in the things they love.

At over one hundred car shows around the country each year, Hagerty employees are on-site, providing activities for classic-car en-thusiasts, such as car valuation seminars, programs for young people to judge car contests (which gets car owners' families involved), and even a place where couples drive up and have their wedding vows re-newed while they sit in their beloved vintage vehicle. Hagerty employ-ees dress up as bridesmaids and groomsmen, and a photographer captures the moment. If that isn't innovative, what is?

At the classic-car shows he attends, McKeel is always thinking about other new ways to build bonds with the people who love classic cars. That's how he came up with the brilliant idea for a unique smart-phone app.

"I've been going to car auctions for years, and a funny thing that I discovered at auctions is there are usually only about ten people in the room actually buying cars, and there are hundreds of people watching the auction as if it's some sort of spectator sport," McKeel says. "They get the printed auction catalog and they wait for the hammer to go down, and then they write in the catalog what the sale price was, their own little tally. And when I noticed everybody in the crowd was doing that, I realized we had an opportunity to create an app to help that process work."

Hagerty Insider is a free classic-car auction tracker app that includes the ability to search cars coming up at auction, review past auction sale prices, and set a watch list for vehicles of interest. There's also an option for classic-car owners to create a profile of the vehicles they already own within the app and to get updates as the valuations of their vehicles change in the marketplace.

"We had about twenty thousand downloads in the first month that we launched!" McKeel says. "Now people can not only follow the auction where they are sitting, they can also see what the sale prices were at similar auctions in the past, plus it covers every live car auction happening simultaneously." The ability to watch concurrent auctions is important in the classic-car world because in January each year, the major auction houses, including Barrett-Jackson, Bonhams, Gooding, and RM Sotheby's, hold simultaneous sales in Scottsdale, Arizona, over the course of a long weekend, and it is impossible to be present at all of them. Hagerty Insider allows classic-car enthusiasts to see what's going on at *all* the sales, and each time they do, *they also see the Hagerty name.*

"We like this idea that you are on the inside," McKeel says. "Owning a classic car is one thing, but knowledge about it is this whole other dimension. People kind of show off and share with one another: 'Oh, did you know that car had such and such an option in 1965?' That's part of the currency around the passion space. Sure, we would like to insure all these cars. But I also want to have people think of us as a hub of building their knowledge to enhance what they already know about cars and just to help them feel better about being a car guy."

As you will now see—he's nonstop! In 2019, Hagerty announced a new community initiative, its most ambitious yet: the Hagerty Drivers Club. For a fee of forty-five dollars per year, members receive a subscription to Hagerty's award-winning magazine, premium access to the valuation tools, invites to members-only events, discounts on select automotive products and services, and roadside assistance, among other benefits. The six hundred thousand existing Hagerty Plus customers are given free club access, and anyone, even people who are customers of other insurance companies, may join Hagerty Drivers Club. "Our goal is to grow Hagerty Drivers Club to six million members," McKeel says. "That magic number represents a 'movement' when nearly everybody knows who you are."

On the minds of some classic-car enthusiasts is the growing interest in both electric vehicles and driverless cars. Many people worry about the value of their investment in cars made fifty or one hundred years ago when the way we get around is on the cusp of major change. The millions of people who will band together around the Hagerty Drivers Club will be a fanocracy to be reckoned with in the debate over rights to the road.

"We expect Hagerty Drivers Club will be a hub and a convener of people who are passionate about all things automotive," McKeel says. "*Together* we have a bigger voice, which will be important as we inch toward autonomy. People who love to drive are going to want to have a say in how people-piloted vehicles and driverless cars share the road."

If you notice, none of these ways of connecting to classic-car enthusiasts—Hagerty Drivers Club, being present at car shows, judging contests, being a catalyst for kids and families to get involved, building an app, and providing valuation tools—directly sells Hagerty's insurance products. What they do instead is help McKeel and his employees build strong personal relationships with existing and potential customers. It builds their fanocracy.

> **Your customers' fandoms can be the foundation of your own fanocracy.**

It's particularly interesting that Hagerty, a company selling car insurance—a product many people say they hate—has developed so many fans. There are many products and services we consume in our lives that are similar, something that we just don't like to spend money on, like web hosting! Ha! Or pest control. Or dry cleaning. Yet creating a relationship-based business is the key to success for *any* industry, even those whose consumers claim to generally detest them.

Hagerty developed fandom around a product "everybody hates," car insurance, and that effort has greatly benefited the company's bottom line. They are now the largest classic-car insurer, with double-digit compound growth since the inception of the business, and in the coming year they expect to add two hundred thousand new customers!

"We went out and expressly challenged ourselves, how could we build fans," McKeel says. "We discovered we're pretty good at it. We have fun doing it, and it matters, because that is our word-of-mouth growth engine."

It's up to us to create what we do around whether it brings people together. To succeed, we must become masters of seeing things from other people's points of view and understanding how other people work independently from ourselves. It's a simple yet powerful concept that any organization can implement.

The idea of building relationships is an especially valuable ingredient for traditional businesses facing growing competition from the rise of digital products and services. Many analysts and members of the media like to point to online shopping leading to the demise of locally owned stores, and the availability of digital music creating major difficulties for those in the music business, including radio stations and record labels. Yes, digital music platforms are tough to compete against. However, as you can see by now, there are major opportunities to thrive instead of succumbing to what many say is an inevitable digital future.

Open House Party: The Radio Show That Beats the Playlist

Some traditional industries face competition from new digital products and services so severe that entire businesses are being wiped out. For example, we can purchase air travel, hotel stays, and car rentals with a few clicks, so what does that mean for travel agents? When a quick search shows the exact price of a car, how does a car dealer skilled at haggling cope? With new ways to consume music, movies, and books, how can existing providers adapt so they don't become extinct?

John Garabedian, the creator and host for thirty years of *Open House Party*, a live show syndicated on hundreds of radio stations as well as available via web streaming around the world, told us, "With music streaming services like Pandora, Spotify, and Apple Beats to compete with, radio needs to offer something more than just songs to be 'sticky' to compete and attract and hold a huge audience." Virtually every major star in the world has been on *Open House Party* over the years, including Madonna, Eminem, Lady Gaga, and Katy Perry.

The essence of the show is a big Saturday night party with music stars joining a small live audience in the studio and listeners calling in live to be a part of the action. Tuning in, listeners hear from the artists, experience the excitement of the audience, and learn about what's hot from the listener requests coming in live on the phone and the web. For many music fans, the excitement of *Open House Party* is much more fun than simply listening to a playlist on a streaming service because of the *interaction with other like-minded people.*

The direction of each show is totally driven by fans because all the music played on *Open House Party* is by listener request. This keeps the show tuned in to what people actually want to hear on Saturday nights. This direct connection with fans means *Open House Party* spots hot new hits first, identifies which songs are the most popular, and, almost as important, determines which songs have died and people have grown tired of hearing.

"Unlike music streaming services that just play tunes, radio needs to sound compelling and fun so that people don't just 'listen' to a show or a station, they actually love a show or a station," Garabedian says. "Great radio gives listeners reasons to be loyal. Outstanding stations attract fans, not just listeners."

Garabedian built a fanocracy of millions of music lovers coming together, listening to *Open House Party* on hundreds of radio stations on Saturday nights. Sure, they may listen to their own playlists on the digital streaming services during the week, but when they want to party on Saturday nights, they tune in.

Rather than give up in the face of stiff competition from online services, people like Garabedian devise ways to build relationships directly with fans. The human connection brings loyalty. For the music fans devoted to *Open House Party*, music is much more than just the product (the songs). Music is engaging with others like themselves to enjoy the lifestyle that music and conversation about music bring. By finding ways to gather people together in live, shared consumption of a product, companies can connect with their fans in ways that digital solutions cannot.

The same approach to building a fanocracy can be deployed at other organizations competing with online product sales. In the book business for example, the rivals to neighborhood bookstores are the online powerhouses that sell at a steep discount and offer free shipping including overnight (or even same day) shipping options. However, what those online services can't offer is the ability to share *personal relationships* with book fans.

Brookline Booksmith: Building an Entire Community of Book Lovers

"I can't tell you how many times I've been at the register ringing people up and they tell me how much they love to visit our store," Peter Win, the owner and manager of Brookline Booksmith, told us. Located just outside of Boston in Coolidge Corner, Brookline Booksmith opened in 1961 with the slogan "Dedicated to the fine art of browsing." Today the store employs forty-five people and operates with seventy-five hundred square feet of retail space.

"It's an amazing thing to listen to people telling you that they like to come spend money at your business! That's just incredible." When we visited Brookline Booksmith on a Saturday afternoon in early December, the store was packed. We counted more than twenty people waiting in line to reach the three cashiers working nonstop. There's no doubt that Brookline Booksmith is thriving.

"Community is really important for lots of small businesses, particularly for independent bookstores because that's what sets us apart," Win says. "We're not just here to sell and restock. We're here to talk about books. Those relationships and those conversations are part of how we build that community. You can get the books and any number of products online or elsewhere, sometimes cheaper. But if you come into our store, you can talk to people about books or you can ask for a recommendation. Maybe you didn't even know you wanted that book. Maybe you've never heard of that book before. You can talk to somebody who says, 'Oh, if you read and like that, then you might try this.' Every day we're having conversations about books and the other items we sell to people from down the street and from all over Boston."

That a physical bookstore is thriving in 2019 says a great deal about how well Brookline Booksmith develops fans. With the rise of online book retailers in recent years in the US marketplace, large physical bookstore chains including Borders and Waldenbooks have disappeared, while Barnes & Noble, the company with the largest number of retail outlets, now operates about six hundred Barnes & Noble branded retail stores down from a peak of over seven hundred, and the company's 797 B. Dalton branded bookstores have all closed. The costly overhead of running a large physical store with many thousands of books in inventory seems unlikely to be a sustainable business moving forward, and yet Brookline Booksmith is still doing tremendous business.

As we were browsing the well-stocked shelves of Brookline Booksmith, we were struck by how many books had "Signed by Author" stickers on the covers. In the front of the store, many of the "recommended" books sported signs indicating the dates the author would be visiting for a talk and book signing. Instead of just selling the product—books—Brookline Booksmith serves as the hub of its local community and facilitates interesting discussions around books inside and outside their store, as their fans talk about their experiences meeting authors and getting advice for their next book club selections.

Win brings in well over one hundred authors per year for events, most happening in the store's basement, where they sell secondhand books. There's something friendly and cozy and warm about a book talk surrounded by tens of thousands of well-loved used books and a gathering of other interested book fans.

"We attract such a wide range of authors and personalities," Win says. "We host writers of literary fiction, genres like mystery, sci-fi, and fantasy, children's and YA authors, as well as cool and interesting non-fiction authors." Win particularly likes when he hosts a new author who goes on to write a big hit. "There is the great experience of seeing a favorite author in a small setting within our store. I remember seeing both Zadie Smith and David Mitchell do a reading in our store several years ago when their first books were published, with crowds of twenty or twenty-five people, which was very good at that time. Now it would be impossible, as they regularly attract hundreds of avid fans." So when an A-list author would like to do a reading or lecture, Win moves the event across the street to the Coolidge Corner Theatre, an art deco movie palace in continuous operation since 1933. Win says, "Authors like Roxane Gay, Michael Ondaatje, and Jason Reynolds have been exciting and have attracted anywhere from two hundred to five hundred or more people."

Occasionally, Brookline Booksmith hosts well-known, celebrity-level authors who are there only to sign books rather than to deliver a talk. "Celebrities tend to attract the largest and most vocal crowds,"

Win says. "In recent years, we've hosted people like Mindy Kaling, Neil Patrick Harris, Andy Cohen, and YouTube star Joey Graceffa, who have done signings right in our store, all of which attracted between six hundred and eight hundred people. That means a line that winds through the whole store, out the front door, and sometimes around half the block. It also means a good amount of joyous screaming, tears of joy, and lots and lots of selfies." And everyone involved—booksellers and customers—are having an interesting experience they will share with others the first chance they get.

Besides selling huge quantities of books at the author events and building a community of people who enjoy being part of these events, there's an additional benefit to Brookline Booksmith, according to Win. It turns out that authors who cultivate their own fans through social media will announce when they are coming to Boston, and their fans go out of their way to come to see their favorite author at Brookline Booksmith. "Many of those authors' fans have never been to our store or never even heard of our store," he says. "The authors' fans get a chance to find out about our store and maybe they become our fans as well."

The downstairs space at Brookline Booksmith is also put to good use by local book clubs that meet there. One of the book clubs has been meeting at the store for more than a decade, and the store maintains a web page for the club that lists the books they've read together. The most fascinating aspect of this club is that it has no affiliation whatsoever to Brookline Booksmith. "Nobody from the store actually moderates or is involved with the club at all," Win says. "It runs itself and they just use our store to meet. It's an opportunity for book fans to come and meet other people who are interested in similar things. That's another way to have conversations about books for us to attract people who want to do that. The club chooses eclectic titles, sometimes fiction, sometimes nonfiction, occasionally something brand new. At the end of each meeting they vote on the next book to read, and they let us know and we bring more copies in. But club members don't have to buy the book from us."

Win is a hands-on owner of Brookline Booksmith. He wants people to interact with him and tap his knowledge, which would be obvious to you if you spent two minutes with him—books are Win's passion. He even publishes his email address on the store's website. "I'm the owner, but I'm in the store myself, I'm selling books, and I work at the cash register," he says. "I am available to anyone in the store at any time. It's important that people know I'm here. We're always trying to make sure that people who enjoy books have a good experience so they continue to be fans of books and this store! They know they can come here any day to find a book and get a great recommendation to find things that they didn't know that they wanted. To be successful these days, you have to be ready to put in the effort into building relationships with customers."

A brick-and-mortar store offers the unique opportunity to create a transformative experience within its four walls. Through obvious curiosity about customers' wants and needs, a traditional store delivers an unparalleled opportunity to prompt customers to not only buy books but also become fervent fans of the unusual experience that led them to their purchases.

The relationships that are built at stores like Brookline Booksmith, with companies like Hagerty Insurance and MeUndies, and among music fans who enjoy *Open House Party* come from creating relationships with people in person, on the telephone, and in clever online communications. As I've said, those relationships build fans who serve as a powerful antidote to what might otherwise be considered "the tough competition."

A genuine interest in your customer leads from transaction to fanocracy.

While many companies falsely think that their job is to facilitate a transaction and to do so at as low of a cost as possible, your job is to create fandom.

Your transition from transaction to fandom is especially powerful when you are dealing with stiff competition that offers products similar to yours. When others are simply selling products, you succeed by creating lasting relationships with those who will become lifelong fans. It requires a genuine interest in your customers, anticipating their needs and wants.

———

The restaurant in Romania that made the biggest impression on me for being all about the relationship could have been just like every other restaurant with great food and a beautiful location. However, the restaurant experience I am about to share was on the top of every traveler's favorites list because of a very different reason. Let me tell you about my memorable experience:

Prior to visiting Bucharest, Yukari and I found it challenging to choose which restaurant to reserve in the city when we were forty-five hundred miles away in Boston. I had a speaking engagement there and was excited that Yukari would join me—we were looking forward to enjoying some free time together in a new and interesting place.

Yukari and I are both foodies—fans of excellent restaurants around the world. It's a fandom I learned from her. Ever since we met, one of her greatest loves is finding an interesting restaurant whose creative chef makes fabulous meals. She has an uncanny ability to remember restaurant meals decades later. When I mention a city we've visited, she'll talk about her favorite restaurant there and what we ate. With that fandom in mind, we checked out reviews on online services like TripAdvisor and consulted an old-school guidebook. Having gone through a similar process prior to visiting dozens of other cities and at least a hundred restaurants around the world, we knew choosing places to eat that we would enjoy could be a hit-or-miss proposition.

A Restaurant in Bucharest

Yukari and I both noticed that one restaurant, the Artist, was at the top of everyone's list, so we booked a table. Upon arriving in Bucharest, we asked the hotel concierge for his restaurant recommendations, and the first one he mentioned was the Artist. We were pleased that we already had a table reserved there.

We were excited as we waited for our Uber to take us from the hotel to the restaurant, and we were delighted upon arrival to see that it is located in a wonderful old villa that has been completely modernized. We selected the tasting menu, which was excellent. We've been to many restaurants with beautifully prepared food in lovely surroundings, but what was the extra ingredient that put the Artist at the top of everyone's list? We needed to wait until the final course to find out.

When it came time for dessert, we were surprised when chef Paul Oppenkamp appeared at our table, introduced himself, and explained that he was there to work with us to make the dish perfect. First, sweet basil and mint were presented within a mortar and pestle. Chef poured a bit of liquid nitrogen into the herb mix, causing all sorts of wonderful clouds and a fabulous hissing noise. He told us to stir rapidly to break down the greenery. Once that was complete, Chef scooped cucumber ice cream into the herbs and told us to stir and eat as quickly as possible. He smiled as we took our first bite of the dessert we made together. Wow!

Yes, the ice cream dish was delicious. However, it was much more than that. The opportunity to have Chef Paul tableside, walking us through the experience, made it extra special. That evening was the most memorable of our week in Romania. It wasn't about the food and decor at the Artist, although both were lovely. It was about our new fandom relationship with Chef Paul!

PART II

Nine Steps
to Building Your
Fanocracy

CHAPTER 4

Get Closer Than Usual

by David

As you might have guessed by now, I love music festivals with dozens of bands playing outdoors over several days, events packed with tens of thousands of people like me, enthusiasts who are thrilled to be enjoying a few days and nights of *live music*! In just a single day, I can catch five or even ten acts, maybe hear an old favorite or two, be exposed to new artists with new songs, and, most important, hang out with my music-loving friends.

At the Outside Lands music festival in San Francisco several years ago, I was particularly excited for the performance by St. Vincent, an artist whose music I enjoyed but whom I had never seen live. Like other large music festivals, Outside Lands features multiple stages with performances coordinated so that when one stage is being readied for an act, there is a band playing on a nearby one. Fans can hear continuous music by walking from stage to stage.

I arrived more than an hour before the St. Vincent set, and I was among several dozen hard-core fans. Other people arrived in a steady stream over the next hour, and when the artist on a nearby stage finished, thousands of people attending that show made their way over to where I was to see St. Vincent.

The show was as good as the reviews of past performances and the YouTube clips. Her white guitar contrasted with the iconic black outfits that front woman Annie Clark, a.k.a. St. Vincent, and her female bass player, Toko Yasuda, wore. The music blended fun electronica-influenced, danceable songs with blistering rock guitar solos. Their unusual choreography frequently included her and Yasuda dancing identical tiny step patterns while not moving their upper bodies for an entire song.

But then something happened.

St. Vincent: How Going Offstage Made a Performance Go Viral

St. Vincent came down a staircase from the stage and played a guitar solo directly in front of me. Wow! She was so close I could have touched her guitar. It was amazing to have the best spot in the entire venue, even better than the pros, to snap a photo on my iPhone. Others around me also captured the moment while the professionals shot over St. Vincent's shoulder to photograph the faces in the crowd behind her. Among the hundreds of live shows I've seen, that moment stands out as unforgettable, and judging from the pure joy of the people around me, the same was true for them too. Even the media photographers were excited because they were able to capture an intimate scene of a great artist with her most devoted fans—those who arrived an hour early for her performance. St. Vincent was down with us for only a minute or so and then returned to the stage. But what a memorable moment! With a few taps of my finger, I shared my best photo on Twitter and Instagram and immediately got a bunch of comments from my friends, many admitting they were jealous. What fun!

When I returned home, I checked out reviews of Outside Lands and learned that St. Vincent venturing into the audience was one of the most commented-on moments in both mainstream media and social media of the entire three-day festival! In fact, the *Rolling Stone* article "Outside Lands 2015: 10 Standout Performances" listed St. Vincent and included a photo of her interacting with the audience, and there I was, right there in the middle of the shot! Bingo! Now when I share this image in my corporate and entrepreneurial group presentations as I discuss fanocracy in action, I always get a laugh from the audience as I joke that I'm not making this story up! It *proves* how big a live music geek I am!

At that performance, the crowd went wild, the show was named as a standout by *Rolling Stone*, and many people shared on social media because of a simple but frequently overlooked dynamic in our digital age: *physical proximity.*

Suddenly I realized this was a factor I needed to examine more closely. It occurred to me that *fandom* is a result of doing what you love, and if you bring forth that passion and share with others, it's possible to create an organizational phenomenon: fanocracy.

Bringing that concept into my talks has been overwhelmingly favorable. People want to share their experiences, and what better place to begin than at work? That's the first place people share where they went over the holiday, on the weekend, or the night before. It's that sharing that creates a common bond, and in some cases, you can introduce someone else to a band, play, opera, or game they might never have been curious about but for your shared enthusiasm.

Degrees of Proximity Make the Difference in How You Connect

What is it about being around other people that drives connection? Why does physical proximity make such a difference? Cultural anthropologist Edward T. Hall has answers to those questions.

Dr. Hall defined humans' use of space in a simple way. As director of the State Department's Point Four Training Program in the 1950s, Dr. Hall was tasked with teaching foreign country–bound technicians and administrators how to communicate effectively across cultural boundaries. His 1966 book, *The Hidden Dimension*, describes the way people maintain various kinds of spatial boundaries—and how this can impact the way we relate to one another in any context, from our relationships with our coworkers to how our cities are designed.

If we want to be effective in our communications, we need to learn how to consciously manage the physical space between ourselves and others.

It's not just a matter of being close or far, or that the closer we get the better it is. Rather, *the significance of each level of proximity can be precisely predicted and managed so as to create the most optimal outcomes.* Hall described "public distance" as more than twelve feet away from others, a distance that lacks any sense of precise interaction among those involved. He identified "social distance" for interactions among acquaintances as being from four feet to twelve feet, "personal distance" for interactions among good friends or family from about a foot and a half to four feet, and anything closer as "intimate distance" for embracing, touching, or whispering.

The most rewarding interactions in our lives occur in our social and personal spaces. Those people sitting near one another at a game or at Starbucks or who are standing near one another in a line at a movie theater or live music show? They're well within each other's social space, and as such each person can unconsciously feel the human connection in a positive and safe way.

> **The degree of human proximity is tied to shared emotion and has an enormous effect on how well we do in business.**

"The work of Dr. Hall is incredibly important because one of the things we're just coming to learn now, thanks to neuroscience, is whenever human beings get together in any kind of situation in the same physical space, their unconscious minds track the locale of every other person in that space even if they can't see them," Dr. Nick Morgan told us. Morgan is president of Public Words, a communications consulting company, and the author of *Power Cues: The Subtle Science of Leading Groups, Persuading Others, and Maximizing Your Personal Impact*.

Morgan's work on how humans interact parallels how fandom cultures form and grow—and how important these bonds are to each of us.

"We're a species that wants to get together in groups of friends, of people that we feel safe with, a tribe, and we want to share our emotions," Morgan says. "We're happiest when we're in social space or personal space with people and we're all experiencing some kind of emotion. We're laughing together or we're crying together. It's why—even in an era when you can watch a football game much more intelligently and closely and clearly and certainly more comfortably on a giant TV screen like many of us have in our homes—people still go to the football stadium. They want to experience the thrill of the shared emotion and excitement. The closer you get within those four zones— for example, from public to social and from social to personal—the more powerful the shared emotions are. That kind of group sharing of emotion is incredibly important to humans and it's been widely misunderstood and underrated by people who have subscribed to individualistic notions of humanity."

People don't want to be alone; they want to be together.

Take note of what Morgan teaches us. *The closer you get, the more powerful the shared emotions are.* The significance of proximity isn't just a matter of convenience or utility, but rather the emotional significance of any given exchange. We're wired as humans to have more emotionally significant responses to people we're close to. And whether we're twelve feet, four feet, or even one and a half feet apart leads to decidedly different emotions.

A fan is who they are not because of a calculated, intellectual decision to follow something, but because of their passion, their emotion, and their sense of enjoyment. To successfully build a fan base out of whatever it is you're doing for a living, or if you want to sell or market a product or service, begin to think of creative ways to develop and cultivate human connections.

Remember the importance of proximity because that can lead you to a better understanding of how to attract and keep potential fans interested in your products or services.

Starbucks: Making Connections to Like-Minded People into a Worldwide Success?

Sure, the patrons at my local Starbucks are enjoying their drinks and they're making use of the free wi-fi. It's certainly a convenient spot to meet somebody. Yes, the seats are comfortable and there's ample parking. Yet a typical Starbucks scene includes perhaps a dozen people, each alone but together with others nearby.

At the same time that we're becoming frustrated with social networks, Starbucks sales have grown from $19.1 billion in 2015 to $24.7 billion in 2018 according to the company's earnings releases. That's nearly a 30 percent increase in just three years. Why is that?

We think it's because Starbucks sells physical proximity to like-minded people.

As an example, one day I met with an entrepreneur at a Starbucks, and she stuck around after our meeting was over, just because she felt comfortable with the other people, alone like her at that Starbucks. While so seemingly common and uneventful, this action actually reveals something of far greater significance. It reveals a simple reason that the woman I met—and many like her—do their work at a place like Starbucks rather than alone, by themselves, at their home office.

The key element missing in our digital world, and the reason Starbucks is thriving, is because of the unquestionable value of something that many people—including the fans with whom I shared a moment with St. Vincent at Outside Lands—tend to overlook. It's something that social networks can't ever provide and are by design meant to bypass. Connecting with people directly is important for all human beings.

A music festival becomes an instant city filled with like-minded people enjoying the same music and being near one another. While waiting for a show to start, we spontaneously form a community, striking up conversations with those around us, secure in the knowledge that we have instant rapport because we share the same interest, and the conversation is smooth and natural, as if we've been friends for a long time. Someone asks, "Have you seen St. Vincent before? What was it like?" Another may join in: "Have there been any other standout performances today? Who are you going to see tomorrow?"

It's not surprising that the live music business is thriving. While CD sales are in decline and revenues from streaming haven't kept up, Live Nation Entertainment, one of the world's largest live entertainment companies, which operates concert promotions, venues, and ticketing, has seen revenue steadily climb for the past decade from $3.6 billion per year in 2007 to over $10 billion in 2017.

Face-to-face interactions enhance your sense of well-being and purpose.

Similarly, Starbucks executives actively cultivate proximity in their twenty-four thousand stores around the world. Indeed, the company tells its investors, "It's clear that our passion for great coffee, genuine service, and community connection transcends language and culture." Starbucks is way more than coffee. The company's success comes from selling comfortable and safe proximity to other like-minded people.

My observations (as well as my own fandom experiences) point to the essential nature of what we all crave from the world around us: being around other people with similar interests. Like those who gravitate to music festivals and to Starbucks, we see the importance of close, nonverbal communication between people as an essential element of all types of fandom—no matter where we are in the world. Sure, concerts include wonderful music, but the opportunity to hang out with friends in a familiar environment is even more important. Comic Con is about a day with thousands of other generous and supportive like-minded fans.

Participants in grueling physical competitions such as Tough Mudder and Spartan Race frequently comment on the importance of the camaraderie of the experience. When others are also struggling to climb that rope wall nearby, it makes them happy even though they're in pain. Participants in book clubs often enjoy one another's company more than the books they discuss. And the personalized shopping experience of a helpful sales clerk often brightens our day and may be more memorable than the clothes we buy.

The Millionaires' Magician: Bringing Audience Members into a Performance

I was seated in the back row as Steve Cohen, the Millionaires' Magician, performed his *Chamber Magic* show in a parlor at the Lotte New York Palace hotel. His show re-creates the salon entertainment that characterized Manhattan during the Gilded Age. To reflect that, the showroom was a beautiful nineteenth-century drawing room decorated with historic paintings and gilt ceilings. Cohen was dressed in a tuxedo, and his guests wore sophisticated cocktail attire. As I sat there, a Vienna palace where Mozart would play for a few dozen people came to mind.

Chamber Magic is a weekend show that's been running for twenty years. The vast majority of Cohen's audience members find the show either by word of mouth and social media from his fans or through mainstream media coverage. For example, in October 2017, Cohen delivered his five-thousandth performance, and mayor Bill de Blasio officially proclaimed it Chamber Magic Day in New York City, which helped interest people who had not heard of Cohen's show.

The parlor seats sixty-four guests, with four rows of sixteen seats each. At both ends of each row, the last four chairs are angled chevron-style, like a half hexagon, so everybody can face Cohen without having to turn their bodies. Those in the front row were two and a half feet away from Cohen. The second row was also relatively close, but the third and fourth rows were twelve or more feet away.

In other words, the audience members from the third row on were in Cohen's *public space*. They weren't near enough to him to build a direct emotional bond. However, Cohen skillfully fixed this. At several points in the show, he involved the members of the audience seated in the third row. Once, he approached a man and handed him a deck of cards to demonstrate a sleight of hand. Several times during the performance, Cohen invited me and others seated in the back row to come up to the front and stand around him and look over his shoulder.

Every magic trick in the show directly involves the audience. Sometimes that means a dozen people or more. Frequently, Cohen moves into the audience, purposefully getting close, to ask us for help. As an audience member, I truly felt part of the show, because like every other audience member, I had an opportunity to be within Cohen's personal space at some point—and I was seated in the back row! Purposefully building proximity into his show ensures the emotional response that creates a powerful relationship with his fans, and this has resulted in two decades of success for Cohen. It was remarkable for me to be able to stand right next to Cohen, responding to his request for "help" during these moments. It was fun! Immediately I felt I was part of the action. I forged a deep connection to Cohen then, and still have one today, years later.

Normally, when we attend a typical stage performance such as theater, dance, music, or stand-up comedy, we're usually in the "public space" of the performer, a distance of twelve feet or more. At those distances, neuroscientists say, our unconscious brain does not track people to learn if they are friend or foe. We don't have or feel a strong personal connection when we're so far away.

While public distance is inclusive of as little as twelve feet, more often with larger stage performances the distance might be one hundred feet or more. In other contexts of daily life such as a walk in a park, there are likely to be many people within our public space, but they might as well be hundreds or thousands of feet away from us, because our unconscious mind doesn't pay close attention to them. The experiences we share with those nearer than twelve feet away, as you can now see, is quite significant.

Building fandom—whether you're an artist, CEO, entrepreneur, manager, politician, teacher, parent, spouse, friend, or other role that involves gaining a closer relationship with others—requires figuring out ways to have other people less than twelve feet away, even *if only for a few moments.* This is something Cohen understands deeply. It's a lesson for all of us.

"I make a point to keep my eye on which people didn't participate earlier," Cohen told us. "I make sure that I get them directly next to me, breathing down my neck, and tell them that now they have the best view in the house. Having the audience this close makes sleight of hand tricks very difficult, but I've learned ways to manage that."

Cohen evaluates the details of every single trick to make certain that opportunities for close proximity with members of the audience happen as often as possible. Recently, he realized that there was a part of a particular routine where he wasn't getting within personal distance of audience members. "It's a trick where I borrow three people's wedding bands and I link them together into a chain," he says. "I ask people to confirm that it is indeed their ring that is linked. To finish the trick, I could easily unlink them myself, yet rather than me being the person doing the unlinking, now an audience member reaches into my fist and feels that the ring is still locked on. I ask them to think the word 'release' and when they have done that, they try pulling the ring again, and this time it comes off in their own hands. That little change of having someone next to me do that action changes the entire experience—people always remember that they unlinked the ring themselves. It gives people what I call a water cooler moment, something to share with others on Monday at the office, where they say: '*I* was the person who unlocked the rings in the show,' or 'Guess who was the one who lifted up the hat and made a giant brick appear? It was *me!*'"

Cohen pays close attention to his audience reviews on TripAdvisor and Yelp and looks for common threads and similar comments. A large percentage of the comments use the words "interactive" and "intimate," so Cohen is reassured that the way he is involving his audience is meaningful to them.

"I don't have a marketing budget," Cohen says. "Everyone who comes into the show, and we've had over half a million people, comes in either through hearing about it in the media or, more likely, through word of mouth. To me, it's not just about the trick. It's about the experience."

Yet we would say that Cohen's performance is all about the *audience*. He's obsessively focused on making certain that each audience member enjoys the special opportunity to be near him. By the end of the show, everyone participates in some way.

That night, I remembered how memorable it was, watching him work the cards signaling the end of the show, when the audience rose up in unison with a sustained standing ovation. At that moment, right along with everyone else in the audience, I became forever a Steve Cohen fan.

Re-creating the Entire Recreational Vehicle Industry

We can't emphasize enough the importance of being together with like-minded people in social space or personal space. For your organization it's the basis for how you communicate to your marketplace. And all it means is figuring out ways to bring your customers *together* so they have the unique opportunity to be within twelve feet of people just like them.

Personal interactions are what makes us human. And humanity is what builds a loyal fanocracy.

That's exactly what the entire recreational vehicle (RV) industry has been doing, pulling together around an initiative to attract younger fans to the RV lifestyle. Here's how their process unfolded:

The recession beginning in 2008 was devastating for the recreational vehicle industry. In 2007, 385,000 new RVs were sold in the United States, but by 2008, sales had plunged to about 200,000. Many manufacturers went bankrupt. The situation seemed dire.

The RV Industry Association (RVIA) started an initiative dubbed

Go RVing. It was a very creative way to build awareness and grow the number of fans of the RV lifestyle. Every manufacturer who is a member is required to pay between $35 and $150, depending on the size of the vehicle, for an RVIA seal on every RV sold. When the consumer buys a new RV from a dealer, the cost of the RVIA seal will be on the invoice and a sticker on the side of the vehicle.

The RVIA has invested between $10 million and $15 million of that revenue per year on the Go RVing advertising initiative. They maintain a website at GoRVing.com and advertise in print media including *National Geographic* magazine. To attract a younger audience, RVIA invests in reaching people on social networks like Facebook and Instagram and on new networks that appeal to their future customers. In 2017 they spent more on digital advertising than on print media and television—that was a first for them. The images they use in their advertising show groups of young campers obviously enjoying themselves. No matter the media, their campaign focuses on the enjoyable human connections, fun, and camaraderie that camping can bring you.

"We say take the family and get out into the campground," Bob Zagami, executive director of the New England RV Dealers Association, told us. "In today's society, many people don't even talk to their next-door neighbor. They don't talk to people at work. We've insulated ourselves from the very people that we need. But when you get into any campground, nobody cares who you are. You're just a person who wants to be outdoors, likes the elements, and likes to be with family and friends. As soon as you pull into a campground, the kids take off and they'll have six new friends immediately. In the next few hours they'll be running around, going on the swings, and doing everything, but they know where you are when they're ready to come back to the campsite. They feel safe and connected with you. You sit down with your spouse and you have a great conversation because *you* know the kids are safe and they're out there having a very good time. And then within a few hours you know the people from the campsite to the right and you know the people on the left because they came by to say hello. You have this personal connection."

Baby boomers have tended to camp in family groups, and the traditional campsite has worked well for them as they have aged. However, the millennial generation enjoys camping in groups of ten or twenty people. "The next generation of RV enthusiasts has already got their social network built out," Zagami says. "Their idea of camping is spontaneous and inclusive. They use Facebook and Twitter to gather friends into groups around a shared experience. They go online and say, 'We're going camping on Saturday morning and we're going to get to such and such a place around 9:00 am, does anyone want to come?' And all of a sudden twenty people show up. They've got like-minded activities that they want to do, and they just happen to do them around an RV or several RVs. There's an incredible transformation from the way that we used to do it to the way that it's done now."

When most people think of camping, they might imagine being in the great outdoors, hiking or fishing, or being close to animals. Indeed, that's what was traditionally the focus when marketing products and services to campers. But research conducted by the RVIA and other organizations reveals that the *social aspects of camping are of primary importance* to people. What makes camping an enjoyable experience is being within the social space of other campers.

The *North American Camping Report*, an annual survey of campers sponsored by Kampgrounds of America (KOA), found that the top reason people want to camp more, cited by more than half of respondents, is *they want to spend more time with family and friends.*

There's something magical about sitting by a fire, telling stories in the proximity of family, close friends, and new acquaintances.

Camping places people in closer proximity than normal for longer lengths of time, and it connects people in unique ways. It's fandom at its core.

Because millennials are so committed to enjoying activity-driven experiences with their friends, camping is an ideal activity for that, and they have become the new drivers of the industry's growth. Overall, millennials comprise 31 percent of the adult population yet account for 38 percent of campers, and enthusiasm is stronger among these younger campers. According to the 2018 *North American Camping Report*, 51 percent of millennials state that they plan to camp more in the coming year. Younger campers are more likely to camp in the largest-size groups, often ten or more people, and say that they are "much more likely" to seek campgrounds that can accommodate their larger groups.

KOA: The Very Social Aspects of Camping Under the Stars

"The whole nature of a campground is that you are social: you're engaging, you're gathered around the campfire at night, and you're making friends from all over just because you happen to be at the same place," said Toby O'Rourke, president of Kampgrounds of America, Inc., when we connected with her. With more than five hundred locations, KOA is North America's largest and most established system of campgrounds. "It's not like when you go to a hotel where you don't talk to the person in the lobby. At a campground you're walking at night and you're visiting with people. You're sharing a beer or talking about the great new rig that they pulled up in, or playing with their dog, or sharing stories. As long as I've been here, we've talked about campgrounds as being some of the last small towns in America. It's a very relaxing social environment."

Besides being with your friends and family, a campground is an environment that makes it safe for people who have never met one another to move across levels of proximity from public distance to social distance with people who share the same interests. It's emblematic of fan culture because it fosters greater emotional significance for all involved.

O'Rourke says that campgrounds are adapting to millennials who enjoy camping in larger groups, and KOA has incorporated more of the things that appeal to them. A particularly popular setup now offered at many KOA locations enables larger groups of friends to combine a half dozen or so tent or RV sites into one compound with a group eating area and communal firepit. It's perfect for millennials who love to camp.

To reach millennials, KOA focuses on marketing through social media, which helps to drive reservations. In particular, they use photos to tell the story of the human connection that comes with camping.

"Our research shows that millennials are camping in larger groups, so we have great group shots," O'Rourke says. "We use real campers in our photo shoots. We never hire models and we've been doing that for years. When we go to a campground we walk around and say, 'Hey, would you guys mind being in some pictures?' and we just photograph people in the natural environment, camping."

Everybody we spoke with in the RV industry mentioned the importance of people being *together* when they camp, being in close proximity to like-minded people. Indeed, the focus on the physical proximity found within the RV lifestyle as well as a deep understanding and adapting to how people of all ages love to camp has produced remarkable results for the entire industry. From a dismal 200,000 RVs sold in 2008, by 2017 there were 504,000 new RV units sold in the

United States, nearly 120,000 more than the 385,000 sold before the recession. This has included everything from small pop-up trailers well liked by millennials to forty-five-foot diesel motor homes costing as much as a million dollars.

"The growth has been staggering," Zagami says. "We can't deliver RVs fast enough. There is a six- to nine-month order backlog and HELP WANTED signs at many manufacturers."

This is a fantastic result for an industry that pulled together to build and grow a fan base merely by facilitating *how people can connect to one another.*

The idea of proximity to customers is something that any organization can implement in order to build the kind of fandom and that creates a true fanocracy.

Josh's Rainbow Eggs: Treating Customers and Chickens Right

Living on a farm in Kerrie, a small town in the Macedon Ranges region of Victoria, Australia, Josh Murray looked after a small flock of twenty-four hens of all different breeds as one of his chores. It was 2009 and Josh was nine years old. His mother noticed Josh really enjoyed working with the hens and told him that if he wanted to sell the eggs, he could keep the profits. Josh thought that was an agreeable idea, so he began collecting eggs and knocking on neighbors' doors, selling his eggs at four dollars per dozen.

Josh expanded his flock and was soon selling eggs at local farmers markets on weekends. "At the Lancefield market, I sold forty dozen eggs in one morning—it was amazing," he told us. "Every few months or so, Mum would hatch more hens and I would have more eggs. The markets in the Macedon Ranges were great, and soon I was at a market every Saturday and covered Lancefield, Woodend, Riddell, and Kyneton too."

Over the next few years, Josh decided to professionalize the operation. The first step was a company name and labels for the egg cartons. Josh says the Josh's Rainbow Eggs name came from a friend who opened a dozen eggs and, seeing the blue and green Aracauna eggs, as well as brown, white, and pinkish eggs, said, "You have rainbow eggs."

By this time, Josh had more than twelve hundred hens and employed people to help him with the chores. He made a significant business leap when he started to sell Josh's Rainbow Eggs at LaManna Direct—Australia's largest 100 percent Australian-grown fruit and vegetable market, with ten thousand square meters of retail space. Josh was now competing with other egg brands for shelf space and customer attention. He was running a *real* business. By this time, he was twelve years old and would go to LaManna Direct many weekends to hand out flyers to customers and talk to them about his eggs.

Josh's young age didn't stop him from acting as a savvy entrepreneur! In 2014, when he was fourteen years old, Josh and his mother met with the national category manager at Coles Supermarkets' head office. Coles operates some eight hundred supermarkets throughout Australia.

"The manager was very supportive and didn't hesitate when we asked about Coles Supermarkets selling our eggs in our local store," Josh says. "Now we are at seven Coles stores, and we also added three Woolworths stores. Our eggs are in nearly every supermarket in the Macedon Ranges and in a number of supermarkets in the city of Melbourne."

By 2017, at the age of seventeen, Josh was selling nine thousand dozen eggs per week at stores throughout the Melbourne area. He's very successful by any measure; however, he still goes to farmers' markets once a month, even though he could easily sell those eggs somewhere else.

Because eggs are for most people a commodity, Josh had a challenge on his hands because his costs were much higher than those of other egg suppliers. His approach to free range was to have just fifteen hundred hens per hectare, whereas other farms typically have far more hens in the same amount of space. But this meant he had to raise the price of his eggs to seven dollars per dozen retail price, while others were selling at just four dollars. Why would a customer spend an extra three dollars for Josh's Rainbow Eggs? How did Josh develop a passionate enough following that his customers would become part of his fandom?

From the very beginning of his business, starting when he was just nine years old, Josh always met personally with customers. He initially sold by visiting neighbors' homes, selling his eggs door to door. These encounters meant that Josh was within four feet of his neighbors, who were delighted to meet the young entrepreneur. A few years later, he focused on farmers' markets, another opportunity to have a personal distance, within four feet, with his customers. Now, as he's been selling thousands of dozens per week, he still makes a point of spending time in the supermarkets that sell his eggs, interacting directly with his fans.

Fandom, the sharing of emotional bonds with others, is a human instinct that is hardwired into each of us.

Josh's experience speaking directly with customers every single week for years taught him that people are willing to pay a premium for compassionate business practices, what he calls "Ethical Eggs." Josh raises true free-range chickens. "Our customers know that we treat the chickens right," he says. "People recognize that even if other chickens are raised on a free-range farm, they are confined and pretty miserable. Our costs are very high, but we're managing to do right for ourselves, for our customers, for the chickens, and for the retailers we sell to."

"Ethical Eggs" isn't just a tagline for Josh's Rainbow Eggs. It's a way of doing business. Josh is very open about how he treats his chickens. While competitors do the absolute minimum to be legally called "free range" in Australia, Josh does much more, and he shares the details with his customers.

"When people buy my eggs, they are walking past far better value in terms of cost when they don't buy the four-dollar eggs and buy mine at seven dollars instead. The customers are enthusiastic about how we're looking after the chickens, and they seem interested in me, in my point of view, and my business."

Compassionate business practices and transparency are good business for Josh. However, it's the direct connection he's made with thousands of his customers that has been the essential ingredient to his success. Because Josh has been within a personal distance of so many customers, he's built fans that have grown his business into a large organization while he's still a teenager.

"I'm doing right by the chickens and our customers," Josh says.

Josh learned from and listened to his fans, and by doing so he created a loyal fanocracy.

Mirroring and Your Fans

So far in this chapter we've looked at the importance of proximate human connection in growing a fan base. People go to live music for more than the show; they go to enjoy close proximity with other people like them. Steve Cohen built a successful career as a magician by building his show so that every member of the audience has a personal connection directly with him, and those audience members tell their friends about how great the experience was. He's performed over five thousand shows and never needs to advertise. We explored how the entire recreational vehicle industry came together to more than double the market for new RVs in a decade by appealing to people's desire to camp in groups. And we spoke with a teenage egg entrepreneur who meets personally with customers and has become remarkably successful as a result.

Let's face it, we humans are hardwired to react to those who are nearby. Our evolution has taught us to unconsciously track those who come near us in order to quickly determine if they are good or harmful. Because these basic instincts are so powerful, when we are close to many people we don't know, like on a subway platform, for example, we're wary. We can't help that response; it's built into all of us. We're preparing to flee or to fight if presented with any sign of danger.

However, when we are in close proximity to people we trust, a personal connection develops. People who cultivate that closeness, bringing customers within a social distance of fewer than twelve feet or a personal distance of fewer than four feet, create strong emotional bonds, and that can create fans.

How can businesses and artists who can't possibly have a direct personal connection with every fan achieve similar success? It turns out that if you perform in front of thousands of people or if your product is used by millions of consumers, you can still use the power of connection. Our unconscious brain can respond to what we see as if it were our own experience, even if it is on social media, film, a screen, or a faraway stage through something called mirror neurons.

Mirror neurons are a group of cells in the premotor cortex and inferior parietal cortex of our brain. These neurons are fascinating because they not only activate when we perform an action—biting into an apple, smiling, or getting near to somebody we enjoy being with—they also fire when we observe somebody else performing the same action. When those around us are happy and smiling, our unconscious brain tells us we're happy, and we often smile too. When we're at a rock concert, our mirror neurons fire based on what the performer is doing onstage *and* what other audience members are doing.

I speak at conferences dozens of times a year, often to groups of a thousand people or more. There's no possible way I can bring each person onto the stage to have him or her be within my personal space the way that Steve Cohen does. Yet it turns out that we humans respond to seeing somebody else having an experience as if it were us. I make it a point to come down from the stage into the audience to interact with a few people in their seats several times during each of my talks. I'm purposefully getting into the personal space of just a few members of the audience, but because of their brains' mirror neurons, others in the audience can feel my presence.

Dr. Nick Morgan, whom we met earlier, says it's like the ripples of a stone being dropped into a pond. "You can genuinely move, touch, and share emotions with everybody in that audience simply by connecting with one or two people. If you move into the audience and ask a question or get a comment, stand next to a person, shake hands with them, interact with them in some way, then your whole audience feels interacted with and the room suddenly becomes very small and intimate."

> **When your customers see you interact with their peers, it's as if you were interacting with them too.**

When you're sitting across from a friend and enjoying a meal, you are unconsciously mirroring their actions. When they reach for a glass of wine, you might reach for your napkin. If they look to the left, you unconsciously look in the same direction because the mirror neurons in the parts of the brain that control eye movement are doing their job. Ha! Who knew?

We were so intrigued by this concept that we wanted to learn more, so we met with Marco Iacoboni, professor of psychiatry and biobehavioral sciences and director of the Transcranial Magnetic Stimulation Lab at the Ahmanson-Lovelace Brain Mapping Center at UCLA and author of the book *Mirroring People: The Science of Empathy and How We Connect with Others*. He shared with us this fascinating concept: "There's this entrenched idea that when I am interacting with you, we are two individuals and there is a feeling of a divide. But in fact, what we see is evolution selecting the brains and the methods that do the opposite, overcoming the division between people, especially when it comes to face-to-face interactions. What mirror neurons really do is facilitate a bond between self and others such that they become two sides of one coin. That gives us an almost magical sense of human connection with others. It's grounded in the body when we interact with other people."

Wow! It turns out that mirroring is not just about those directly across from you. An important aspect of mirroring is that the brain fires even when the other person is far away, like during my speeches, or even a virtual presence on a screen. This mirroring helps to explain both the positive and the negative aspects of social media. We can relate to people via images on their Facebook and Instagram posts. Our brain tells us we're close to them because of the photographs or the video they share. Perhaps that's why social networking posts with photos and videos of people tend to have many more social interactions than those with just plain text, and more interaction such as likes and shares than those with photos and videos that *don't* feature people.

"There are many mirroring processes going on when it comes to social media and it certainly facilitates an understanding," Iacoboni says. "When I see you posting something on a social network, especially on visual networks like Instagram or Facebook, it triggers in my brain all sorts of imaginative processes, so I can understand you from a more human standpoint, not just based on the things you're saying. However, when there is no face-to-face connection on social media, people lose that magical connection and that makes it easier for people to get into an antagonistic way of relating to other people."

As a live music enthusiast, I have been fascinated with how the science of mirroring helps to explain why I am passionate about going to concerts. What Iacoboni said reminded me of the time a few years ago when I was dozens of rows away from the stage at a Rolling Stones show, and a simple hand slap that Mick Jagger shared with a lucky fan far away from me lit me up too! Apparently, as Iacoboni suggests, the mirror neurons in my brain reacted as if Jagger had given me a high five. It was an unforgettable part of that show!

People unconsciously bond with actors and artists and speakers they see on-screen and onstage because of mirror neurons. Mirror neurons also help to explain why we feel that we "know" movie stars and television personalities. Our brain tells us that we've been in their personal space because of the feeling of proximity to them that we get from seeing them up close on the screen. That explains the successful reaction that fans have to stories and magazine articles about and interviews with their favorite performers.

"An artist can't get close to everybody in the audience," Iacoboni says. "But just being close to some audience members builds a sense of oneness between those people who are close and those farther back. Members of the audience fill the gap between the artist and them in terms of distance and space, and when we see a performance, we can imagine the musicians performing the music and empathize with them and mirror neurons are very important for this. To be a more successful artist requires a process that includes both a bottom-up imagination that you mirror your own fans and what they like and then transform that into a top-down plan for transforming your act in a way that will lead your followers."

A critical aspect of understanding mirror neurons is to remember that it's how we're hardwired. It's our ancient brain at work helping us to cope with the world around us. It's not something we can choose to turn on or choose to ignore. It's innate. *We can't help ourselves to react in the way that we do.*

For musicians, public speakers, teachers, politicians, or others who command a stage, the presence of mirror neurons means that our audience will be more connected to us if we call upon a couple of people throughout the performance to be in our personal space. You can move into the audience several times. You can ask people a few questions and gauge the percentage of responses by a show of hands. Think about choosing one or two members of the audience who raised their hand to ask a simple question by walking over to them and into their personal space. Ask them to elaborate on the answer they gave, and present them with a handheld microphone for their answer. This simple act will get you into a few dozen people's social space and a handful of people's personal space in a natural way during your presentation. If you have the opportunity to be in front of a large audience and you're being broadcast on large screens, even people thirty or fifty rows back can see the interaction, and mirror neurons fire in their brains too, as if you were speaking directly to them.

A deeper understanding of mirror neurons can help you build fans of your organization. Create your own fanocracy by understanding your audience and learning what *they* need and want.

Celebrity Selfies Are the New Autographs

Bradley Cooper shot a selfie with a gaggle of A-list actors as Ellen DeGeneres hosted the 2014 Academy Awards telecast, and she tweeted it out live via her @TheEllenShow Twitter feed. It injected fun, real-time quirkiness to an overproduced event. In the photo, the actors aren't posed as you usually see them. And it's not a paparazzi shot. It's just people—it was DeGeneres and Cooper and Jared Leto, Jennifer Lawrence, Meryl Streep, Channing Tatum, Julia Roberts, Brad Pitt, Lupita Nyong'o, and Angelina Jolie—worming their way into a photo just like we've all done. That one moment added a great deal of humanity to people who because of their celebrity seem untouchable; the selfie moment suddenly made it seem like the actors were touchable, real, and intimate.

The photo proved to be so popular with fans that it brought Twitter's servers down for about twenty minutes, and by the end of the Oscars broadcast it had become the most retweeted tweet ever. As we write this years later, that selfie has 221,694 replies, 3,390,679 retweets and 2,383,784 likes.

Is there another, even more powerful reason why we are so attracted to this moment?

A selfie taken with another person or several people is one of the very few times that people are permitted to get into the intimate space—within one and a half feet—of others. Unless you're a loved one, there just aren't many socially acceptable times to get that close to other people. A crowded elevator is another example, and while elevators are a socially acceptable place to be in one another's intimate space, most people would likely agree that it's not a comfortable way to ask strangers to join you in your selfie. (Well, maybe the *first* time it might be a little uncomfortable . . .)

The selfie demonstrates something significant to us because of the orientation of our bodies when we snap a photo. While the two (or more) heads are typically well within intimate space, the subjects of the photo are actually facing the same direction. We are in intimate space because we have to get our heads close together. However, because we're oriented in the same direction, we're aligned. This alignment becomes a powerful expression of wanting the same thing as that other person—even if it's only for a fleeting moment.

Some see a selfie as frivolous and childish, but that's outdated thinking. Selfies are a very powerful and immediate way to share emotion. Imagine if two people who didn't trust each other were a foot and a half away. If they were facing each other, they would likely feel awkward or threatened. But when two or more people face the same direction, such as looking at a camera, it's acceptable. The humble selfie breaks the intimate proximity barrier! It is safe *and* enjoyable.

Asking for a selfie with a famous person can be a casual way to be close without being intrusive. Years ago, asking for an autograph served the same purpose. Requesting and shooting the selfie gives us a chance to briefly get near our sports hero, our favorite author or actor, or the person who might be the next president of the United States.

Asking for a selfie is easy because the worst thing that can happen is the celebrity may decline. And if they do, you are not worse off than before you asked. Win or break even.

A selfie creates a permanent record or a keepsake. I like to shoot selfies with people I meet, like the one I took years ago with astronaut Neil Armstrong, the first human to set foot on the surface of the moon.

Here's a suggestion to anybody reading this who is frequently asked to pose for selfies: Do it with pleasure! It builds a forever passionate and instant fan base, one person at a time.

I had an opportunity to ask a presidential candidate for a selfie and noticed that she had a wonderful approach to granting requests of the dozens of other people patiently waiting to do the same. She would take the person's smartphone herself, find the best angle, shoot a few photos, and hand the phone back. She was adept with the smartphone. Her approach to selfies was amazing—maybe seven seconds a person—shorter time than if nervous fans were fumbling with their own phones.

And who was this person with such an efficient selfie strategy?

None other than Hillary Clinton.

I asked Clinton about her approach, and she told me she figures she's shot tens of thousands of selfies over the years. By personally shooting the selfies, she not only gets through the rope line faster, she also gives her supporters something to share on social networks. "Hillary Clinton took this photo herself!" It's a lighthearted and fun fan-building technique that impressed me.

———

We can't begin to compare the difference between interacting with friends on a network like Facebook and interacting with people who are actually sitting next to you. In the gigantic social experiment that we're living today, using mobile devices, while having limitations, is incredibly powerful. You can develop your fandom today by being in close proximity to others and sharing that proximity with other people you can't be near. Have fun!

CHAPTER 5

Let Go of Your Creations

by Reiko

In a converted warehouse in the Chelsea neighborhood of Manhattan, I came upon a forest. The eerie rolling fog obscured my vision as I peered out of the hallway to the dense grove of trees. Just beyond the shadow of the blue, moonlight-like glow, I spotted movement. A figure was watching me from another doorway, another hall, his or her mask visible for the briefest moment before it disappeared and left me alone in the trees. I took a breath, taking in the silence in this dreamlike place. I stood motionless until I heard strands of music swell and grow behind me, and I felt it was time for me to move on. I turned and traveled deeper into the strange maze of touch and smell and sound.

Sleep No More is a fully immersive work of theater adapting Shakespeare's *Macbeth* to a 1930s-era world. The British theater company Punchdrunk has transformed five floors of what they call the McKittrick Hotel into forests and graveyards, private bedrooms and public shops, and an asylum and dance hall. The performance takes place simultaneously throughout the whole building, while the audience members are given masks and encouraged to follow whatever part of the story they desire. The whole story, from start to finish, cycles three times over the course of a night, so any one audience member can see a similar scene from another angle or find another thread of plot on a different floor or take their time to get lost in secret rooms behind false doors.

About halfway through the night, I followed the stumbling steps of a character as he hurried down the stairs. His was a frantic dance, two steps up and four steps down. Then, like a hound that had caught a scent, he rushed forward in a sweep and I ran after him. Who was he? Banquo? Macduff? Digging through my fraying memories of *Macbeth*, I followed him as he burst through a final door and into a dimly lit room.

When I entered, I stopped short. The room was set up as a banquet hall, with high ceilings and room enough for the many guests that had gathered. The man I had followed here climbed the steps up to a table on a stage, taking a seat facing the gathering, and I was reminded that I was still watching a play, not living a dream. That *they* were the actors, all on that stage, and around me in a bigger crowd that I had seen all night were the rows and rows of masked audience members.

And suddenly I realized what I was seeing in front of me. The culmination of *Macbeth* and what each thread had led to—the finale. But the thing was, I must have missed this scene the first time. I knew it had happened already because there were some scenes I had seen twice, but somehow, in my exploration, I had missed this final decisive plot point. The death of Macbeth. How could I have missed it? What else had I not witnessed? The careful map of events I'd been plotting in my mind fell apart.

Sleep No More: Facilitating Individual Interpretations of *Macbeth*

It was in that moment I realized I had still been trying to experience this play like I had the many others I'd seen on Broadway—from start to finish, careful not to miss a single thing—but *Sleep No More* isn't meant to be experienced like that at all. Though I was surrounded by other members of the audience in this New York City play, we were free to move and interact and explore.

There was always more to see. There *will always be* more to see!

I realized I had been watching the performance, until that point, as though it were my job to find the single answer to this story, but going about it this way would never work. There were too many threads and too many discoveries. I left the banquet hall without a sense of closure that the end of a play normally brings. Instead, I experienced the excitement of a new beginning. As the audience scattered and the story started another cycle, I set out in search of a new character to observe. I knew there were infinite numbers of ways I could experience this show, this night, and still call it *Macbeth*. I was here to see this story anew, excited to see what I could find.

Sleep No More is masterful at playing into the desire of audience members to shape their own experiences—to dive deep into what they find most fascinating or mysterious or beautiful. It never forgets, never tries to pretend that the audience isn't there and watching and participating in the creation of their own story. I found I didn't feel betrayed by the production when I realized I wasn't seeing everything, because the story didn't compel me to enjoy it a certain way. We, as audience members, were rewarded for being curious. For thinking and interpreting and choosing what to look for next.

The success of *Sleep No More* highlights an exceptional idea that many creators overlook—*the importance of encouraging the vastly different experiences from a single work.* Each scene is different and holds different clues to the puzzle of the production as a whole. The experience itself begs you to come back for more. To think about it, talk to others, and then return with new eyes ready to explore and view it differently. It builds a playground rather than a static product with beginnings and endings.

The minds behind *Sleep No More* are tuned in to their audiences. By observing the variety of experiences of their plays by their audiences, these creators also gain a deeper understanding of it, and are able to take their work to new and greater heights. As they say, the plot thickens.

When I stepped into the McKittrick Hotel, I had expected a simple theater production, but I left with questions and ideas and awe. I left with more excitement than I had come in with.

It isn't trivial for a work of art to inspire a spark of inspiration in another. I wanted to talk about what I had seen, as well as what I didn't. I wanted to match up my previous readings of *Macbeth* to the performance I'd just witnessed and think about how my view of the centuries-old play had changed. I wanted to interact. The success of *Sleep No More* is its willingness to serve that desire and delve deep into the vastly differing knowledge bases that the audience walks in with. They "get" their audience.

In any endeavor, creative or professional or somewhere in between, we have a personal, psychological investment in its being well received. In our personal lives, we wait with bated breath as we send our résumés to future employers or spend hours constructing an email with the perfect balance of confidence and humility. We want our work to go over well. On the larger scale, companies spend endless brainstorm sessions around conference tables discussing customer service and the best way to launch a product. Quality improvement, marketing strategy, careful front-facing staff—these are all valuable and necessary components to ensuring our creations stand on the best legs possible out in the world, but they also have the side effect of distancing creators from how the work lives and is received and experienced in the real world.

In development meetings, it's usually the "ideal consumer" that's discussed. The smiling blond girl in the ads who will adore her new doll, or the rugged craftsman who builds his own furniture with power tools. Yet behind the closed doors of their offices, they don't see *who* really uses their products and *how*. Or a person might be on a stage or platform giving a talk, and they aren't walking through their audience and really listening to and seeing up close what the reactions are.

By market estimates, the majority of young adult novels are purchased by adults many years older than the intended audience. Though female gamers are seen as a novelty in marketing campaigns aimed toward men, in the United States the actual gender breakdown is close to evenly split, with women making up 45 percent of people playing video games. Or consider how financial firms market retirement investment services. They are marketed to older couples with the cliché ad image of a happy, fit and fiftyish, his-and-hers salt-and-pepper-haired couple doing something active like mountain biking or hiking. It's as if younger people don't save for retirement and single people don't either. By staying behind closed doors, those companies are not going to find out what those nonobvious customers want: they don't see the range of adults who read YA fiction or the vast number of women playing video games, and miss completely younger or single or LGBT people saving money and planning their futures.

Those account for thousands, if not millions, of fans who are missed.

Even when there are systems in place designed to connect the company to the customers, there are major opportunities that are ignored. Help phone lines and feedback services take the loudest and most extroverted consumers one at a time. Many people are talking to each other, but not to the company of people who can take the information and put it to good use. Groups of beta testers and first viewers add the positive element of discussion but are often not representative of the whole population of fans that will be interacting with the work.

Why is genuine insight so hard to get? Just think about how the layers of policy and formality distract from how readers or users or consumers—fans—really react to your products and services. The true voices of the people who care the most about the creations are lost somewhere behind company jargon and PR.

Adobe: Failing to See Through the Customer's Eyes

Adobe Systems, the computer software company, made the mistake of ignoring fans. I've used their photo-editing software for years for visual art and often take to the internet to find tips and strategies from other artists—things like layering techniques, brush-styles, and art tablets that work well with Photoshop. One day while searching, I stumbled on an artist's blog making fun of Adobe's website. The link took me to a page on Adobe's website explaining exactly how to use the trademarked term Photoshop. This reference to Adobe trademarks, intended for businesses using these trademarks for marketing purposes, reads like a high school grammar teacher reprimanding a student. Here are a few samples below. See what you think, or better, what you would do instead.

Trademarks are not verbs.
Correct: The image was enhanced using Adobe® Photoshop® software.
Incorrect: The image was photoshopped.

Trademarks must never be used as slang terms.

Correct: Those who use Adobe® Photoshop® software to
    manipulate images as a hobby see their work as an art form.

Incorrect: A photoshopper sees his hobby as an art form.

Incorrect: My hobby is photoshopping.

Trademarks must never be used in possessive form.

Correct: The new features in Adobe® Photoshop® software are
    impressive.

Incorrect: Photoshop's new features are impressive.

I just laughed! They sounded so detached from the very fans who
pay hundreds of dollars to use their software, many of whom write and
read the kinds of blogs where I found the reference. Every incorrect
statement sounds like a fan of Adobe Photoshop software, while every
correct statement sounds like a robot. Not only that, it's condescend-
ing. It's an insular, top-down approach that makes no effort to understand how their real fans use the software. Why didn't they just tap
into their huge network of artists and designers that already talk about
their product and listen to what they say, and then ask some questions,
get into a dialogue?

**Some companies are so focused on telling customers
how to enjoy their products, they miss the fan-made
culture that has blossomed around them.**

What *Sleep No More* does that separates it from other plays in New
York is not simply letting their audience walk around the stage. It allows

us, the viewers, to play a major role in the construction of the narrative. It allows us to experience the story from different angles. In return, the actors react to how we move and what we do, paying attention to the many individual ways we see the story unfold. The freedom deepened my experience of the play. I gained insight on how I personally watch theater as well as a better understanding of Shakespeare. The production is there to facilitate and to lead, but never to control.

> **Deepen your understanding of your own work by seeing it for what it means to a fan.**

In any type of creation—personal or professional—the greatest insight is gained from seeing it from another person's point of view.

What Is Fan Fiction?

I'm a proud author of fan fiction. When I was growing up, it was easy for me to fall into online worlds. There are currently over 3 million works across twenty-five thousand fandoms on Archive of Our Own, one of the largest fan fiction hosting websites where fans can post, comment, and share fan-written works. The site, run by and for fans, works like a library for fan fiction where anyone can search for stories by fandom, genre, rating, or hundreds of other categories. I loved Harry Potter and, *oh, look!* I could find pages and pages of stories that allowed me to never leave Hogwarts. I could relive book one from Hermione's eyes or I could see what Harry did after he graduated. Then I started writing my own stories, diving deep into how I imagined the magic system worked and a variety of ways the characters could have defeated Voldemort. One story I wrote blossomed into a full-length novel—a retelling of the seventh book, except Draco Malfoy is a spy for the Order of the Phoenix, working against Voldemort.

I asked a question, *What if . . .* and my keyboard helped me find the answer.

However, when others asked what I'd been doing all weekend, locked in my college dorm room typing away, I answered vaguely. "Writing," I said, because whenever I explained further, I got blank stares and shrugs.

Some authors might assume fan fiction is trivial or even damaging to their careers. There are too many examples of rigid creators trying to control their own fans, even going so far as to belittle readers for daring to interact with their works in this transformative way. Anne Rice, the author of the Vampire Chronicles, said, "It upsets me terribly to even think about fan fiction with my characters," and requested that all her fic be removed from the online platform fanfiction.net. "Every fanfiction I've read to date . . . had focused on changing the writer's careful work to suit the foible of the fan writer," another fantasy author, Robin Hobb, wrote. "That's not flattering. That's insulting."

Even in subtler instances where the creators comment on their work to set the record straight, they interfere with how fans think for themselves. Harry Potter author J. K. Rowling, in a now famous interview after the series concluded, announced that her character Dumbledore was gay. "If I'd known it would make you so happy, I would have announced it years ago!" she said. However, it's interesting that she didn't make that obvious in her books. I didn't notice any clues slipped in to allow readers to fully understand her character in that light. Instead, she acted as if her defense were more meaningful than her words on the page.

For many years I was embarrassed that I cared so much about fictional people that I devoted hours and hours of my life to unraveling their inner demons. I hid behind pseudonyms on forums online because I didn't want my "real-life" friends to know what I was writing. Was it so strange? There were millions of people in the community online, so surely they shared my passions.

Check, Please!: More Than a Comic Book

At 2017's New York Comic Con, in the bustling chaos of the Javits Center, crowded between booths and the continuously moving sea of costumed fans, I stood in line waiting to meet a creator I'd admired for some time. I am a fan of Ngozi Ukazu for her writing and illustration work, and also for how adept she is at conducting herself in the multilayered interactive world of her fan base.

She writes the webcomic *Check, Please!*, about Eric Bittle, a collegiate hockey player who loves baking pies and is terrified of checking. It follows Eric (called Bitty by his teammates) over the years as he grows closer to his team, hones his abilities on the ice, and falls in love with his team captain, Jack.

It might not be what you think of as an instant bestseller, but physical copies of the second volume of her comic earned the most crowdfunding of any comic ever on Kickstarter, with more than $100,000 raised in the first hour of her campaign and more than a quarter of a million dollars overall. She also has over fifteen hundred active patrons on her Patreon subscription platform, and First Second Books offered *Check, Please!* a two-volume publishing deal. Her first book came out in 2018.

I was only one of many in line at that Comic Con waiting to see her.

What makes this comic so popular? Ukazu seems to have found that perfect point between engaging with her fan base and letting it thrive on its own. She's tapped into the sort of story that my generation is yearning for—filled with LGBT characters, people of color, mental illness, fluffy romances, and humor. She also listens to and understands that her work inspires creative energy in others, and so she encourages it.

Ukazu takes a multimedia approach to her creation as well as her interaction with fans. She posts her comic on her website while simultaneously blogging responses to fans and updates on her Tumblr and keeping an in-world Twitter account "run" by Bitty himself over the span of the comic's timeline. Fans can interact with each of these aspects of her world as they please, reblogging or retweeting or commenting on what she has posted. "The stories that developed and the reader interaction added an extra layer of narrative to the webcomic and made people feel like Bitty was real," Ukazu says in an interview with *Entertainment Weekly*. The heartwarming story set up in this interactive fashion made the *Check, Please!* fandom grow fast. On Archive of Our Own there are more than six thousand works and growing, with more art and other fan works on other platforms like Tumblr and Twitter.

I saw up close the genuine joy she channels into her work and her fans when I made it to the front of the line and got a chance to talk to her. Her smile stretched wide across her face as I picked out a sketch zine for her to sign. She fumbled a little with the cash—she was working alone at her booth and was acting as author and manager at once—but nobody behind us in line seemed to care that she spent a personal few minutes with each fan. They knew that soon they'd have their own time with her. She was gracious and generous.

"Who should I draw?" she asked as she picked up her marker.

I asked for my favorite character, Kent, and we chatted about school and living in the Northeast as she sketched.

In her years of work being curious, and meeting and engaging with fans like me at conventions and sharing with us online, Ukazu has gained a deep understanding of exactly what her fans like and dislike. Through conversations with us, her fans, she learned of things she never would have otherwise considered. She listens, gains insight, and when she stumbles, reacts quickly. The result is a better product, something both she and her fans are proud to be part of. By creating relationships through shared interests, Ukazu has created her own fanocracy.

What Ngozi Ukazu has done so well in her development of *Check, Please!* is her awareness and encouragement of the transformative side of her fandom. Not only does she allow her fans to actively engage in her world, despite the fan works changing what she has done in the comic itself, she celebrates it. The very depth of her understanding of how her fandom works comes from her knowledge of the independent creations her fans make based on her comic, and she enjoys discussing fan theories, or *headcanons*.

The *Check, Please!* fandom grows because fans get to create their own stories.

Ukazu says on Den of Geek that finding her "healthy relationship" with fandom took time to accomplish. "My biggest advice for creators is to leave fandom alone. Appreciate it, but don't try to control it. Similarly, readers should understand that headcanons might never be canon and the story and characters belong to the creator. End of story. The relationship starts to deteriorate when one party tries to control the other."

That's the case with any relationship, right?

West Side Story, Hamilton, and Other Classics Transform Older Works in Interesting Ways

Fan fiction is more ubiquitous than many assume. You may have recently watched or read something that could be categorized as such. Here are few examples you might be familiar with.

The Aeneid is Virgil's fan fiction of the Homeric epics, taking a minor character from *The Iliad* and filling in his story. Many works of modern fan fiction do this same thing—take a character the audience isn't told much about and expand their background using textual evidence as well as imagination. Like Virgil did by referencing *The Iliad* and *The Odyssey* in his poem, authors are often careful about how they fit their beloved characters into canon, or the original text. For example, someone writing fan fiction on the TV show *The West Wing* might want to write about Josh Lyman's life after the conclusion of the show.

Dante's *Inferno*, while we're on the topic of myth, is an example of a *self-insert* fic. Dante, a character in his own story, meets the shade of the poet Virgil, who takes him into the underworld. Modern writers play with this idea as well, from Stan Lee cameos in Marvel movies to television's Larry David in *Curb Your Enthusiasm*.

The musical *West Side Story* is a *modern-day alternative universe* (abbreviated "AU" in fandom) of Shakespeare's *Romeo and Juliet*. Same familial dispute, same star-crossed lovers, with a little more brick and metal in the cityscape. We have a vast array of television shows that are modern-day AUs of Sherlock Holmes that remove the characters from Sir Arthur Conan Doyle's original Victorian setting. These include the BBC show *Sherlock*, the CBS show *Elementary*, and the Fox show *House*.

Other AUs seen in fandom range from the ubiquitous *coffee shop AU* to the historical *Regency-era AU* to the *college AU*. How would Romeo and Juliet's story be different if they met on Tinder? What would Sherlock Holmes be like sitting in a university physics class?

The musical *Hamilton* is a *race-bent* retelling of the Founding Fathers. While it has been criticized for being historically inaccurate, the Pulitzer Prize–winning show in fact takes liberties with its cast and timeline to comment on the intersection of America's history and modern-day conflict. As a Creole bastard born in the Caribbean who then went on to become the first US Treasury secretary, Alexander Hamilton mirrors the dreams of many throughout America. Then, by portraying his story with a cast mainly composed of people of color, Lin-Manuel Miranda shows how the United States is still continuously shaped by the people who come to its shores seeking their version, their own interpretation, of the American dream. Miranda uses history because he's a fan of the past—then changes it because he lives in a complex present.

Fans who are free to take ownership of part of the universe you've created take what you've done to a realm you never thought possible.

Miranda's experience as the son of Puerto Rican parents shaped how he viewed America's history, which allowed him to write *Hamilton*. Many authors of fan fiction are the same, using their individual experiences and beliefs to shape their understanding of canon to create—to comment on, to explore, to share what they saw—whether that be through race-bending history or dropping characters into coffee shops to talk things out.

When fans take ownership, it doesn't mean that they take away power from the creators, because it isn't a zero-sum game. Rather, by transforming and adding their layers of understanding, fans are expanding the scope of the original work, propelling it further, reaching far more people than it could have reached before.

Hot Rods and Land Rovers

When I was young, my dad took me to classic-car shows. He owns a restored 1973 Land Rover Series III 88 hardtop, and once in a while, in the summer, we'd wash the car until it shone and then drive it to a field where dozens of other old trucks were lined up. I was six years old, riding on my dad's shoulders as he took me around to see the other vehicles, pointing out the similarities and differences and explaining the history of each. He knew the trajectory of the Land Rover brand from its development in the United Kingdom after World War II. And he talked about how the bodywork of the early models was handmade from an aluminum and magnesium alloy, because at the time steel was rationed and those first vehicles were painted only in the light green of the military surplus supplies of aircraft cockpit paint. Most of the time, I didn't understand what he was saying, yet I enjoyed watching him discuss the intricacies of the brand with the other owners. His eyes lit up as someone opened the door of their truck for him to look inside, and then he'd invite them back to ours.

My dad's love of vintage Land Rovers, from the nuance of their history to the details of their restoration, is curatorial, or as many in the fandom world call it, *curative*. Though these elements of his interest take place far away from Land Rover's marketing department, they are still tied to the detailed intricacies of names, dates, and numbers. When these cars are judged at independent shows, they are scored from the perspective of accuracy to the original and care of restoration. Like a museum or private collection, these fans carefully curate works in their original forms. Curative fandom is what most people are comfortable with. In fact, it is the focus of heavy marketing from industries. It's the accumulated knowledge and physical medium of a work—the trivia, the action figures, the baseball cards, the tell-all autobiographies—that define curative fandom.

On the other hand, there are many other car enthusiasts who love the *transformative* category of car fandom. They build hot rods by starting with a base car, stripping it down, and building it back up as something far different from the stock model vehicle they started with. For example, the long-standing lowrider communities in Southern California disassemble and create something beautiful, traditionally from Chevrolets. However, that auto transformation has nothing to do with what the powers that be at Chevy say or do. This is what is called *transformative fandom*. These fans take inspiration from one work that moved them to create something new—they transform it. For cars, this means building and modifying, yet it can take many forms, such as fan fiction, fan art, fan-edited videos, parody songs, and many others.

Understanding the different ways these fans choose to interact with the source material is key to any business. Neither curative nor transformative fandom is superior, but each has different needs. Often, curative fandom is what companies understand, and indeed the only aspect of fandom they market to, but being able to tap into both can be much more powerful.

The Voice of the Reader

This transformative way of interacting with media is not new. Roland Barthes, French philosopher, linguist, and critic, wrote an essay in 1967 entitled "The Death of the Author." (In fact, in the original French, *la mort de l'auteur* is a pun on *Le morte d'Arthur*, referencing another piece of literary fan fiction, Sir Thomas Malory's Arthurian tales.) In this essay, Barthes argues against the prevailing mode of criticism at the time that put the author at the center of the conversation. Instead, he insists that the meaning of a text does not come from the author. The author loses control of meaning as soon as the work is out in the public because as each reader has a different background, each brings their own context to interpret the work. *Meaning* is what comes from personal reactions to words on a page.

Stanley Fish, another literary theorist who works in the "reader-response" movement, goes further to say that without the reader, the text doesn't exist. Instead, Fish argues that *interpretive communities*, the subjective experiences and influences of each reader, are what ultimately shape the interpretation of any text. One episode of a TV show such as *Game of Thrones* can be experienced in a widely different manner if you are a feminist theorist, someone interested in CGI, or someone who knows everything there is to know about the history of Western fantasy from Arthurian legend to *The Lord of the Rings*. Readers can belong to many distinct communities at once, depending on their life experiences, and these communities are constantly changing.

Meaning comes from a web of influence rather than one static idea. It comes from thinking both about the CGI and the feminism in *Game of Thrones*. Fandom is one way of sharing our infinite meanings or distinct interpretations of creative works with one other, thus shaping our readings of the canon. We use fan works as a way of communicating our meaning, or interpretation, of what we enjoy with other fans—a narrative form of literary analysis. Just like Lin-Manuel Miranda shared his reading of American history through a lens of immigration and race, lesser known fans posting stories on Archive of Our Own share their own readings using the lenses through which they see the world. The environment of sharing is to everyone's benefit as it deepens and morphs our own understanding of the media we love by seeing it through one another's eyes.

What is the difference between fan fiction and the shaped and re-woven texts from *The Iliad* to *Macbeth* to *Frankenstein*? Is it really about the meaning of the stories, or about *who* is telling them?

The authors of fan fic posted online are overwhelmingly female. Archive of Our Own, in a self-conducted survey, found that more of their respondents identified as genderqueer (6 percent) than male (4 percent). On the other end of the spectrum, professional creators are overwhelmingly straight white men. A 2016 study of diversity in entertainment by USC Annenberg examining the gender and racial makeup of those who worked on films, TV shows, and digital series found that women made up 3.4 percent of film directors, 10.8 percent of film writers, and 33.5 percent of speaking roles. In the same line, just 7 percent of films depicted a racial or ethnic balance that was within 10 percent of the true balance of the US population by census. *Because many people in the fan fic community can't find stories that represent who they are in traditional media, they write their own.* It was common in fandom to portray Hermione Granger from Harry Potter as black far before the English actress Noma Dumezweni was cast for the stage production *Harry Potter and the Cursed Child*. The desire for stories about queer relationships is one of the driving factors of the multitude of gay romance fan fiction. Fandom is where many people from marginalized communities can control their own consumption of media, transforming it to make it a more enjoyable and nuanced experience. When the majority of what we watch is from a male perspective, online communities give us an outlet to subvert those cultural narratives. Like Lin-Manuel Miranda, we take the works we love and create works that reflect our points of view.

> **Fanocracy is built on the experiences of all its members, rather than limited to the imagination of one creator.**

Letting go is a technique that we can use in all businesses and professions to build a fanocracy, because fan ownership of ideas is a powerful tool to spread the work. The professional also gains the most valuable feedback process ever created—the ability to see what their creation looks like from someone who has lived a completely different life.

Ubisoft: Embracing Fan Creativity

Video games are one type of media that lends itself well to fan ownership and community building. Multiplayer games encourage teamwork, and role-playing games delve into player choice and independence. Fandoms of games grow around strategy and sharing of experience; however, this occurs more for some games than others. In this rapidly growing industry, there is such a range of types of gameplay and scale that companies constantly try to figure out ways to create long-term fans. With so many new titles coming out one after another, what can drive someone to become loyal?

Tommy Francois, VP of editorial at the video game publisher Ubisoft, understands this dynamic between fan and creator well. Ubisoft is the fourth-largest publicly traded gaming company in the Americas and Europe, climbing the ranks from their small beginnings in rural France in 1986. With a market capitalization of over $3.5 billion, the company has achieved success due to their cultivation of well-known titles such as *Assassin's Creed, Far Cry, Prince of Persia*, and *Rayman*. Ubisoft was also one of the first video game developers to embrace the fan communities surrounding their games. They believe it to be a major factor in the continued success of long-running franchises. Francois explained that it takes many levels of planning on the creator's end to achieve a positive dynamic between players and the brand—involving marketing, communication, and the specifics of game development itself.

Since 2006, Francois has been in charge of developing new franchises, supporting studios through the creative process, and thinking of new, innovative ways to bring the video game medium to new fans. He thinks a lot about the power of fan communities and the gaming company's role in guiding their experiences—both on and off the screen, when to step in and help and when to let fans create their own journeys.

Many of Ubisoft's current games are *open world*, meaning that a player can choose where to go and what to interact with in a larger virtual playing field, rather than being limited to a singular story line. Francois likes to describe these sorts of games as a mix of sports—a set of rules from which stories can be built—and Greek myth—with the overarching knowledge of a canon and history in the context of the environment. Players have agency in the simulations built by the game designers, and fostering this creativity, argues Francois, is essential to building a fan base.

"For us it's key in building simulations that it's a unique medium of expression, so it's all about losing control and letting the fans take over," Francois told us. "The more the fans surprise us by using the simulation in new and innovative ways, the more it's a tribute to how we didn't let it be a designer's game. Instead of feeling dumb because you didn't understand what the designer wanted, the alleged 'proper way,' now, it caters to your intelligence."

This feeling of accomplishment, of ownership of their experience, also drives fans of Ubisoft games to talk about these games more to their friends, in person and online. Gaming systems make this easy with share buttons that connect to social media now a part of controllers for the PlayStation 4, Xbox One, and Switch.

"A part of this geek culture is about bragging rights," Francois says. "If people are sharing, it's because they feel they're unique and creative and are problem solvers."

Fans post videos on YouTube or tweet their successes because they want to spread the news of their accomplishments and the feelings they experienced while they achieved them. This is true not only of video games, but many other industries as well. We take pictures of the three-layer cake we baked from a recipe online to post on Instagram, or we record our best 5K run on smart watches to send to our friends. Every day, we share our little successes (and some failures—I've never been a great baker and have videos to prove it), and with each act of sharing we spread our fandom in the process. We build our own fanocracy with other fans who like what we like.

"Branding isn't about a million facts. It's about emotion. Characters can change and then the story changes. If you get what people loved interacting with your world, that's the brand. That's why data isn't the answer to everything," Francois says. "It's not a designer imposing a feel, it's infinite emotions to one situation."

Fans want to interact with one another at Cons because they've spent hundreds of hours playing together online and want to see each other in the flesh. Fans want to create because they want to capture those infinite emotions and express them in a way to communicate with other fans. *See? This is what this game has done for me.* That is the power of a brand with a true fanocracy. In the collective creation that happens within a company, serving the community is what sets your brand apart.

Fans share their experiences because they're motivated, inspired, and excited.

The team at Ubisoft found a way to successfully make their fans happy—through their fan communities. Again, just like in the game, in the real world the game creators can't be in control of the actions of their players. "When you're working with creatives, to them, it's about having ownership of their ideas. I think it's the same with fan communities. They need to be owners of their tools, of their websites, of their blogs, and now we enable it. We give them the means," Francois says. He sees fan work, including fan fiction, videos, and the work done to improve these fan communities as positive things that creators shouldn't get in the way of.

"It's something to be proud of, for creators. We invite them to shows. We make it part of the celebration and cosplay is a perfect example of that. It's not just a disguise. In most instances it's months of designing an *Assassin's Creed* fan video. We've actually made it part of our marketing. We completely embrace it. For us, we could never put any friction on something like that." Ubisoft invites fans to be a part of the development process from early on, inviting ambassadors or star players to conferences such as E3 to speak with them and thank them. *Each one of these fans reaches hundreds or thousands through their work in fan communities,* and so by interacting with these fans seriously as individuals dedicated to the games they play, Ubisoft can help the community as a whole. "It's much better for us to work on vectors or amplifiers than trying to control."

What is the one piece of advice Tommy Francois would give to anyone who wants to create a fanocracy?

"Love your fans because it's the only way your fans will love you back."

Star Wars: Backlash and Rules of Engagement

The distance between creator and fan is growing thin. We can contact our idols on Twitter and be vocal about what we love or hate in online forums. Throughout the internet, harassment is a problem. The vocal minority of a fan base sometimes goes too far, and creators can be cruel right back. So how do we follow Francois's advice and love our fans while still allowing them to have the freedom to disagree with what we have done? There needs to be a way to balance interaction with individual expression.

For example, Kelly Marie Tran, an actress in *Star Wars: The Last Jedi,* deleted all her photos on Instagram because of harassment from fans of the franchise. They sent her sexist and racist taunts and threats because, in their eyes, her character did not fit into the world they knew as Star Wars. Daisy Ridley, another Star Wars actress, also distanced herself from much of her online presence for similar reasons.

They both chose not to deal with the sort of fan engagement that tells *creators* what they should and should not do within their work, including casting women in starring roles.

As a result of the actions of a subset of Star Wars fans, the community as a whole lost the fun and insight of creators who enjoyed interacting with their fans. While on the opposite side of the coin, letting go is an issue facing the fans as well. In the wake of the vitriol, many Star Wars fans wanted to step away from that vocal minority, some from the franchise as a whole. *Solo: A Star Wars Story*, the next movie out, tanked at the box office. Fandom is not a monolith, and the disagreements that come up can be toxic to both sides who fail to see from the other point of view. Fans will fast leave communities that they no longer feel welcome in, and creators will often put down projects that cause them more pain than pleasure.

Some fan communities have made an effort to set rules and guidelines within a governing system to keep fan activities accessible to all. The Organization for Transformative Works (OTW) is the nonprofit organization run by and for fans that hosts Archive of Our Own. To protect the diversity of fan experience, the OTW does a lot to ensure an exchange of ideas persists among disagreement, including holding elections for board positions and enforcing terms of service with content and abuse policies. Even further, they run a legal advocacy committee dedicated to promoting balance and protecting fan works.

The Power of Engaged Business Communities

Part of fostering an open and inviting environment for fans is dealing with backlash. It takes time to find the sweet spot of interaction and freedom, and even then, creator and fan need constant adjustment to understand their place and that the results are better than what either can do alone.

We are able to learn a lot about this balance of power and freedom from community organizations in business.

The three basics to building a strong fan base are the same:

1. Know your audience.
2. Give your communities the correct resources and space.
3. Always treat your customers as humans.

"Always start with your audience. The who dictates the how, where, when, and why," says Vanessa DiMauro. She is the CEO of Leader Networks, a strategic research and consulting firm that helps companies use digital and social technologies to gain competitive advantage. "Too often, organizations pile on the content when they're building a community. They shove everything they've got into it and never think about the humans who will use it. That never goes well."

DiMauro has worked to build online communities with organizations such as Cisco Systems, Hitachi, and the World Bank. Her company does in-depth research on what both leaders at the companies and their users want in terms of customer service and communication channels to implement sophisticated online consumer communities centered around the product or service. The goals of Leader Networks' work with their clients are much like those at Ubisoft or even the Organization for Transformative Works—to support open communication within a fan base and empower those in the community to be free to do their creative or professional work in a safe place. For these companies using DiMauro's expertise, an interactive user or partner community is an unrivaled advantage. Encouraging user sharing of ideas deepens the knowledge base of the company because they are more in tune with what their customers like and dislike, and what they should focus on next.

From the very start, when building a community, DiMauro says organizations need to bring customers into the creative process. "There must be an involved group of core members—ambassadors or friends of the firm—that partner pretty heavily with the organization in the social design of the community." These early engaged users will model behavior on communication, knowledge, and collaboration to set the tone and culture. Then, the company must slowly transfer authority and agency to the community. As DiMauro explains, "The goal is to move from 'sage on the stage' to 'guide on the side.' You can't let the community completely run itself, because members don't have the backend data and knowledge. The ideal state is when the organization that sponsors the community acts on behalf of the community while balancing the goals of their organization."

DiMauro categorizes core members of online business communities into three different types according to what drives them: First, the *experts*. These members are often consultants or tech wizards who enjoy sharing what they know because it will build their own businesses. Second are the *connectors*. These members are professionals and devotees who are in the community for the interaction and camaraderie. Third, the *disenfranchised*. These members come to the platform only to solve a problem they can't solve on their own.

Understanding how each of these three different groups contributes to online interaction will allow your company to establish a stable, helpful community. According to DiMauro, "When brands design to understand their customer, to solve their problems, to meet their needs, to delight them on every front they can within reason, then the outcome will almost invariably be customer loyalty and advocacy."

> **Once you put your art, product, or service out into the world, it's not fully yours.**

In the past, marketing departments were charged with being the voice of the customer. The company was always in control of the message, and agency was taken away from the consumer. With online communities and public forums, this is no longer the case. If marketing professionals cling to the old ways by charging themselves with being the voice of the customer, they will miss what really matters to their fans.

Microsoft: Partner Networks and Peer Communities Grow Business

Kati Quigley, senior director of marketing communications at Microsoft, offers similar advice from her work with the company's worldwide partner program—a digital and in-person community of three hundred thousand partner organizations with a total of over 1.5 million individuals. The partner community is a critical aspect of the Microsoft business because it generates $95 billion in annual revenue, a significant percent of its overall business, through its robust and constantly evolving partner ecosystem. While it is tempting to try to control the message to partners, she says she knows that "you don't always want to hear from the company that is trying to sell you something. You want to hear from your peers." It is important to give these partners the freedom to say both positive and negative things about Microsoft because "when they do say something positive, it's authentic. It's something that people pay attention to."

Quigley reminds us that people are going to talk no matter what. It's the nature of the hyperconnected world we live in. We leave Yelp reviews or send out tweets when we have strong emotional responses, good or bad. Our peers are the ones we pay the most attention to.

"They truly are the ones doing the job every day, so they have a lot of credibility and a lot of understanding of what it's really like to be a Microsoft partner, and what are the challenges and how they overcome them to find success," Quigley tells us. "It's one thing for Microsoft to say what it's like to be a Microsoft partner, but we have a very different perspective. And so hearing from their peers—truly what are the things they need to know, what are the things they need to learn, and how do they go about it—is so valuable."

Creators can't control every individual's opinion, but they can open a space where fans interact.

Letting go doesn't always work the way the creators, or other fans, want. This extends to policing what is said in these communities. DiMauro says companies have to step back. "The *only* true communities are the ones where people can say whatever they want," she says. "Once organizations breach trust and eliminate the social capital of the community, then people stop talking. To succeed, you've got to create a safe space."

It takes time to find that place where you can let go of your creations, yet still understand the heart of your fans. You may make mistakes, but building mutual respect between fandom and creator, each in your own space, will ultimately be the most rewarding. Live up to their love of your creation and respond, but don't smother them with your ideas of what your product is. Think instead about what your product *could be* once others add their meaning to yours.

No One Way to Tell a Story

In that Manhattan warehouse turned 1930s hotel, I experienced *Macbeth* like I hadn't ever before. As soon as I shed my idea of what it meant to see a play and embraced the transformative nature of *Sleep No More*, I found myself falling deeper into the story than I could have otherwise. I followed my curiosity to a child's bedroom and discovered a false mirror that revealed a murderous scene on the other side. In a room set up as a bar, I spent a few minutes playing a game of chance against one of the characters, picking cards he laid out on the table. I stepped back in a scene where I'd been before, watching from the far wall so I could take in the broader view of the action.

When I left, I took with me the stories—what I'd touched and smelled and smiled at—and shared those stories with everyone around me. First, to my husband, Ben, who went with me that night, though we were sent in separate directions as soon as we entered. Inside, we had only fleeting glimpses of each other. He had a different experience, saw different characters and scenes, and found different puzzle pieces in the secrets of the production. Later, I shared stories with my friends who shared my love of literature and theater.

In an interview with directors Felix Barrett and Maxine Doyle in the official program for *Sleep No More*, they were asked if there is a best way to experience the show. Barrett's answer is this: "There's no one right way to do it. Just trust your instincts—everyone's response is different."

Indeed, there is no one way to enjoy art or media or product. Every time *Macbeth* is put on, it is an interpretation. The key to the audience coming back for more is allowing space for that interactive transformation to take place. Let them want to see it from a different angle or in a different light.

As a company or a creator, all you have to do is build a playground that others want to play on. Then let them go play.

CHAPTER 6

Give More Than You Have To

by David

I t was time to paddle back out.

I had just surfed for the first time on the North Shore of Oahu, Hawaii, where surfing was pioneered. Somehow, I had managed to ride the wave to the beach, vaguely aware that a few of the others were evaluating me as they paddled back out. No style points earned for sure, a bit dorky actually, but no wipeout. I had made it! I had actually surfed the North Shore!

Though I had learned to surf in Australia twenty-five years earlier, my worry on the North Shore had been about the locals. Hawaiians are known to be very territorial about their waves. As they should be. This was and is the best surf on the planet. Many others like me come in for a few days, some rudely invading the territory the locals rightly consider their own. It's important to respect the locals because they are also the ones who cultivate this area, this culture. They surf this wave every day, while for me it was the first time.

Normally I'm focused on the waves. Instead, I paid close attention to who seemed to be the alpha dogs, those who had status because of their surfing ability or because they were at their home wave and were well known. I was merely a haole, the Hawaiian word for "foreigner."

And as a haole, this was my game plan: hang back to show my passivity.

My passive strategy seemed to be a good one, because no dirty looks (or worse) came my way. I was ignored.

After paddling out for the second time, I was there in my outside spot once again, focused on how the other surfers related to my own lowly position at the very bottom of the hierarchy.

Watching the locals take their waves, I waited, hoping for another big set to clean the lineup to have another chance. Remembering my ride made me smile, sitting on my board and hoping for another yet content with my experience on the last wave. I would always remember it.

Another set rolled in and a bunch of surfers got their waves. There wasn't one for me, so I waited some more. Then a couple of good waves came toward the lineup. Clearly nothing for me because others were in position. Moving wasn't an option.

That's when it happened!

A Hawaiian surfer was in the perfect position to take one of the oncoming waves. Yet he very clearly backed off. What was he doing? Then he turned around, looked me in the eyes, and nodded. It was just a tiny movement. Barely perceptible. It was kind of a sideways nod, maybe an inch or two of head movement. If I hadn't been focused on him, it would have been easy to miss it.

He'd given me a wave. *His wave!*

Unbelievable!

Paddling into what was now my wave, smiling again—somehow managing to get into the pocket without embarrassing myself—was the thrill of my week! And because the other surfers couldn't see me over the top of the wave, my poor skills didn't matter.

Dead last in the pecking order.

Nobody owed me a thing.

My position was clear to me and everybody else. Because I was never expecting to be given a wave, nothing had prepared me for it. I may have come into this experience more concerned with being a haole, yet that was no longer the case.

This amazing Hawaiian surfer gave it because he wanted to.

This experience changed my perception of this beautiful island, of Hawaiians, and of surfing in this hallowed place. His gesture even changed my perception of my place in the universe of surfing, from an invisible pretender to somebody worthy of a wave.

For him it might have been easy to give the wave away. He'd already taken around a dozen waves that day, and many thousands over the years. It was just one wave among many for him. Yet for me, it forever sparked the memory of a lifetime.

On that day, I became a fan of the North Shore of Oahu. And this was because of what that surfer did for me. It's something that brands can do for would-be followers to turn them into devoted fans, something that inspires passion in others.

With that wave, he gave me a gift. And he expected nothing in return.

The Incredible Power of a Simple Gift

In our fast-paced world, everyone is constantly bombarded with offers, opportunities, and opinions. Those of us seeking passionate followers of our brands and other contributions have to sift through everything and somehow create a substantive connection. The cluttered nature of the digital age means that we have a mere fleeting moment to leave an impression.

When we have only those few seconds, most people and the organizations they work for act as if by shouting louder, using brighter colors, or making their web pop-up more intrusive, they'll succeed in getting someone to stick around. They assume that if they fight even harder and more ruthlessly for the attention span of would-be followers, they'll "win."

Doesn't this sort of arms race leave us all defeated?

However, we can learn something from that surfer on the North Shore of Oahu. On that day, he gave me a wave. Yes, on the one hand it seems easy to simply dismiss the gesture as frivolous, something not worth mentioning. And for him it probably was. For me, though, visiting the North Shore for the first time, it was surreal. In the same waters I had only seen in online videos and in my surfing magazines, that wave was epic!

Even more, that gift had a profound effect on me because it was completely unexpected. Instead of my being intimidated by the alpha-dog locals, one of them completely turned that perception upside down. He transformed my personal feelings about surfing in Hawaii. I went from being nervous to grateful for the experience of surfing in the most famous waves in the world. I became a fan! I *am* a fan!

From an increasingly fast-paced bombardment of offers through an ever-growing array of media platforms, our connections to others are more and more virtual.

As we dig ever deeper into our digital lives, we grow increasingly disconnected from other humans. As a result, we have even less time to determine whether someone is going to help or take advantage of us.

Do you feel as though you always need to be on guard? Are you thinking some nefarious organization is trying to steal your personal data? Can you trust this organization enough to give it your credit card number? Is this person on social media who they say they are, or are they some bot or scammer?

We scan things to figure out in a moment if it holds value for us, and if that value doesn't jump out right away, we move on to the next thing. We don't think about the fact that another human being created that which we are considering. If we do choose to consume it, we try to complete that transaction as quickly as possible so as to, again, move on to the next thing. And when we offer something to others, we often create a mental ledger where we only provide it when we get something equal or better in return.

If our digital disconnect is the problem, doing what that surfer did for me that day offers a simple and powerful opportunity. We break transactional patterns by doing the opposite of what's expected.

When we give to others rather than take, we develop a fanocracy.

This solution to developing a fanocracy is inspired by an unlikely source, one based on my intense fandom around live music since I was fifteen years old.

The Grateful Dead: Giving Away Music to Reach New Fans

I first became aware of the idea of giving away something of value as a way to build a fan culture when I was a teenager. I was (and as I've said I still am) a live music geek, at that time attending rock concerts in the New York City area with my high school friends. There was one band that developed fandom in a unique way. Unlike all the other musical

groups whose tickets or signs at the venue read NO RECORDING AL-
LOWED, the Grateful Dead encouraged concertgoers to record their
live shows.

As I mentioned in the opening of the book, the Grateful Dead is my
favorite band, and a big part of the reason is how they treated fans. The
Grateful Dead was the first band that realized they were selling music.
Not records, not tickets, not T-shirts. Music. And one of the best
ways to sell music was to get as many people exposed to that music as
possible.

Initially the people recording shows set up their tall microphone
stands anywhere they liked in the venue. "It started to become a problem because people were complaining that all the microphone stands
were harshing their trip" (disrupting their view of the stage), said Bob
Weir, Grateful Dead founding guitar player and vocalist. "So we decided to make a designated recording area." That recording area meant
that all the people making recordings were in one place at the venue,
so they weren't disturbing others at the show. "The tapes got around.
They got copied, and copied, and copied. By the time it got beyond the
third generation, there was an awful lot of hiss on it. So that's only going to whet your appetite. You're going to want to go see a show or buy
a record without all that hiss on it and we put out numerous live records. What we found is that it served as promotion and it worked very
well for us."

The Grateful Dead gave the gift of free music taping, and it turned
the community into a fanocracy.

The Grateful Dead's gift of permission to tape shows introduced
new people to the band who heard the tapes in dorm rooms, apart-
ments, and cars. Many of those new Grateful Dead enthusiasts then
wanted to see a live show too, generating hundreds of millions of dollars in ticket revenue to the band. Indeed, the Grateful Dead was the

most popular touring band in the country during the peak of its career in the late 1980s and first half of the 1990s. Surviving members of the band touring as Dead & Company in 2019 are still selling out stadiums and arenas across the United States, more than fifty years after the group formed in San Francisco in 1965.

Every other band said no to allowing the taping of their concerts while the Grateful Dead said, "Sure, why not?" The Grateful Dead created a fanocracy by allowing their fans to freely create recordings and share their work. This delivery of free content, fan-recorded and fan-copied cassette tapes, built a social network of enthusiasts before Mark Zuckerberg was even born.

With the rapid growth of the web as a place to share content starting in the mid-1990s, music fans suddenly had the ability to share music from any band via free download sites such as Napster. The recording industry feared file sharing and banded together to shut down these sites, making it illegal to download music.

Yet the Grateful Dead continued their tradition of allowing the trading of live recordings even after the death of Jerry Garcia in 1995. In 1999, the Grateful Dead was one of the first bands to allow free downloads of their fan-recorded live performances via MP3 and similar file formats. Soon the Grateful Dead live music section on Archive .org included over ten thousand freely available concert recordings.

The Grateful Dead gave away their music in the same way as the Hawaiian surfer gave me the wave, with no expectation of something in return. Fandom is built on human connection, and when you're given something of value completely free and with no obligation, you tend to share your appreciation with others. Fans copied and shared countless millions of Grateful Dead recordings when each of them passed on the gift of a cassette tape or download link to other fans. And all of this led back to the band that made it happen. It was a true fanocracy with a huge tribe of Deadheads financially supporting the band for decades by buying tickets to their live shows.

Really, Truly, and Completely Free

What is most interesting about the example that the Grateful Dead set through its tradition of giving gifts is how it extends to many aspects of the surrounding community—even beyond their shows in particular. This provides us with a valuable insight into the power of such a culture and the value of fanocracy as a whole.

At the Gathering of the Vibes music festival I went to several years ago, I particularly enjoyed wandering around the camping area. It's fun to encounter interesting people who are part of the same tribe, those who enjoy grooving to the same musical vibe.

There were a bunch of tie-dyed shirts on a low fence, and I figured that somebody was selling them. Tie-dye is very popular at Vibes and had been a staple of Grateful Dead shows for decades. As I paused in front of them, the man standing nearby told me they were free.

Now, that's interesting! I thought.

So I got to chatting with the man, Dave, who made them, and he invited me to take one. Dave told me he loves to make the shirts, and giving them away brings back much more to him than charging money ever could.

By giving away free tie-dyed shirts, Dave said he meets interesting people. He initiates meaningful conversations. He gets interesting gifts in return and gives back to the community.

The shirts really are free, and Dave's cool if you simply walk away with one. In confidence, he told me some people actually ask what they can do for him. He always suggests making a donation to the Vibes food drive.

There was a cool purple and blue shirt (with a pocket!). I had to pick it up and told Dave I'd be right back. I went to my campsite, grabbed a copy of my book *Marketing Lessons from the Grateful Dead*, returned, signed it "for Dave," and presented it to him.

He was excited. It was a great trade for both of us. Two music fans gave each other something of value that made the quality of both of our lives better.

While the Grateful Dead set the tone decades ago for this kind of community by allowing its fans to record its concerts for free, this story about the T-shirt demonstrates a very important point that runs in tandem with the larger idea about the importance of expecting nothing in return. When someone like Dave expects nothing in return, someone like me is far more likely to actually offer something in return.

When "Free" Becomes Coercion

The ability to create and share content on the web means that any organization can use this technique pioneered by the Grateful Dead. A great way to build fans of your work is to give away free content such as blogs, videos, white papers, infographics, e-books, photos, and the like. In the online world, it is so easy to give away content—much easier than tie-dyed shirts!

Dave's T-shirt was truly free. While I was eager to give him a copy of my book in return, he didn't demand or expect anything from his gesture. Yet the idea of "completely free" is particularly tough for business-to-business (B2B) companies who are eager to trade content such as a white paper for an email sign-up registration.

A gift can also be a powerful way for a business to build fans, yet most marketers misunderstand the *nature of free*. Instead of offering something like Dave did, with absolutely no expectation of something in return, nearly all organizations' "free" offers on the web are actually demands for something. In this case, the consumer's personal information.

The white paper online registration is a holdover from when white papers needed to be delivered by postal mail. It is a technique that was developed for the days when direct mail was a primary driver of new business. There are many people who believe they can derive value from a registration gate on content; if they capture an email address from that person downloading the content, that person then becomes a sales lead. A target.

The problem with gating content is many people won't bother to register for privacy reasons. They don't want an email or phone call from a salesperson. Another problem with gated content is there is very little sharing on social media because people don't want to expose those in their social networks to possible spam.

Making content like white papers totally free without registration means that the content spreads, Grateful Dead–like, as far as possible. Value comes from many more people being exposed to the content via social networks.

I've spoken with hundreds of marketers who offer content as a way to generate new business. Most require registration and some don't. It's a religious debate much like creationism versus evolution. You can't win the debate. Each side believes they are right, and it is impossible to see the wisdom of the other side. In the religious debate regarding content, I am firmly in the "totally free" camp, yet many marketers feel equally strongly about the value of email sign-ups as a trade for content.

The good news is a few marketers have conducted "A-B tests" of the same offer as completely free versus one with an email sign-up requirement and shared their data with me. Those companies tell me that they get between twenty times and fifty times more people who download free content versus gated content.

It's clear that if you want to spread your ideas, free content is the way to go. Sure, some people will just take, and others will share the love with their friends, colleagues, and family members by posting about your content on their social network or emailing a link to somebody who would find it interesting. This sharing of your gift of content helps to spread your ideas and grow your fan base.

We frequently hear from people who say that if you give away your ideas "for free" via web content, people won't have a need to buy your products or services. However, many organizations have successfully used this approach.

Free content with strings attached feels like coercion—while great content given freely attracts loyal fans.

I recognize from having worked with companies over the past decades, including many in the B2B world, that the pressure from management to generate leads is frequently so great that marketers can't offer free content like e-books and white papers even if they want to. They are told to use content to generate sales leads instead.

That's where a hybrid offer comes in. A hybrid offer is a lead-generation method that takes both religious views into account. This method includes an initial offer that is totally free to people who do not yet know you or your business. Then, within the initial free content, you include a secondary offer that requires registration that you can use to capture leads. A secondary offer might be a webinar that is related to the content in your white paper and educates or helps people more.

An added benefit of this hybrid approach is the difference in leads. The gated content approach simply generates email addresses from people who want your initial content offer. The hybrid approach, on the other hand, generates email addresses from people who have already consumed your initial free content and now want more information about your company and your products and services and are eager to learn more. With most lead scoring systems, the hybrid model leads will be hotter than the white paper leads.

You might ask, What if you are a company selling a commonly used product to consumers? How can your organization cultivate fans?

By now, the answer may not surprise you, yet the source of that answer possibly will.

Duracell PowerForward: Giving Away Millions of Batteries to People in Need

Many organizations offer products and services that seem to a consumer to be very similar to another offering. With common products such as household goods and office supplies, people usually choose the least expensive option, forcing many companies to offer coupons and special sale prices to entice customers to buy.

Most people think that low-cost option rarely builds brand loyalty. Fickle consumers are happy to ignore your brand of yogurt or toilet paper or bottled water or copy paper when there is another brand offering a better deal.

Some consumer products have developed a powerful brand based on expensive advertising campaigns. Yet, like the constant discounting, investing in expensive ads is also a tough way to build a business because of the need for constant reinvestment in a costly overhead.

An alternative approach is for brands of common products to give gifts to build fans.

Natural disasters like hurricanes, tornadoes, and floods are happening more frequently every year, causing power outages for millions of people. Duracell, a company best known for alkaline batteries in many common sizes, assists those in need through its PowerForward program. The company helps affected communities across the United States by sending out company-branded trucks to distribute free Duracell batteries, provide mobile-device charging services, and offer internet access to those without power.

Yes, Duracell is giving away free batteries. Literally tons of free batteries! And it is an incredibly powerful brand-building program.

A team of ten people from Duracell PowerForward helped Puerto Rico's 3.4 million American citizens who were left almost entirely without electrical power by Hurricane Maria. Duracell airlifted two trucks and over thirty tons of batteries to give away to those in need. *Thirty tons of free batteries.*

"Every time there is a power outage, battery consumption and demand spike," says Ramon Velutini, VP of marketing at Duracell. "With hurricanes, tornadoes, floods, and powerful storms occurring more frequently in the US, there are a lot of people who need our product at a very critical moment. People need batteries and everyone knows that, so they go out to buy batteries but generally batteries run out. We saw that the first brand to go out of stock was always Duracell because people think of Duracell as a brand of battery they can trust and that is very much for real when a critical moment like a storm hits. But it's troubling because even though people want to buy our brand it is not available."

The Duracell PowerForward program began in 2011 with one truck, and now there is a fleet of five trucks. The sole purpose is to deploy quickly to affected areas and distribute free batteries at the moment of the most critical need. The team has responded in the aftermath of over forty-five weather events all over the United States.

Duracell uses Facebook to provide real-time updates of where the trucks are as they head down to the village level. The Facebook posts are incredibly active as people request batteries to their location and offer thanks to Duracell for being there. Right after the hurricane, I made notes about the reactions in Puerto Rico: there were more than 30,000 likes, 11,500 shares, and many thousands of comments on the Duracell Facebook posts about PowerForward in Puerto Rico. Most were in Spanish, and here is a taste of what was being commented on in English:

VELIA GOMEZ: I met 3 days ago one from the team. Keep up this great initiative and thank you

KAT MARRA: Thank you Duracell you guys are amazing

VIVIAN GARCIA: Duracell thank you! You don't have to do this, it's a great thing that you're trying to accommodate everyone one city at a time!

And then there are interactions between the affected and Duracell employees:

MARIA M PEREZ: What about Humacao, are you planning on visiting our town, which was totally destroyed as many others by Maria.

DURACELL: Our goal is to travel through as many areas as possible, stopping wherever we can.

"If you think of our brand promise as delivering power you can trust, then the tone and character of the brand is to deliver this power when it really matters to people," says Velutini. "This program is just perfect because it is the literal delivery of our brand promise to consumers. It's a fantastic sweet spot of delivering power when it matters and building relationships on a very personal basis with consumers."

As we were speaking with Velutini, interviewing him about Power-Forward, we found it amazing that when the demand for his company's product was at its absolute peak, when everybody wants batteries, when there is a black market and price gouging by some, he directs his team to give the product away for free!

We wanted to know about the internal challenges around making the batteries available at no cost. Does the company try to calculate the return on investment (ROI) of giving away millions of dollars' worth of product? With most corporations run by people with business school backgrounds focused on turning a profit every quarter and meeting short-term financial goals, what Duracell has been doing is considered radical. Aren't there people inside Duracell (on the financial side perhaps) pushing to deploy the trucks to *sell* the batteries instead of giving them away for free?

"It continues to be a debate," Velutini admitted. "But the debate always ends when we deploy our PowerForward team and we start seeing the pictures of those who we're helping, and we start hearing the stories. The reality is that this is an investment in the Duracell brand. There are a lot of brands that just say good things and try to take a stance at a certain moment. And there are others that do a lot of good by donating money. But we feel that the best way to help is to take action and when people have an experience on a personal level with a brand, the dividends will pay out forever. On social media, where we do measure, PowerForward is constantly the number one most engaged thing that we put out every year. The PowerForward content always outperforms on an engagement basis compared with everything else, so we can take that as a proxy for getting to a return on investment."

Velutini shared a story about a mother who approached a PowerForward truck and requested many batteries in all different sizes. Since this was an unusual request—most people just ask for several batteries of one size for a flashlight or small radio—the team asked about her situation. The mother said she had a three-year-old with more than ten disabilities: "He needs batteries for his ventilator, he needs batteries for his dialysis machine, and you guys came in the perfect moment and I and my family will be forever thankful for that," she said.

"So we were able to provide power in a time of need for a mom with a son with that situation," Velutini says. "Our product plays a huge role in his life. What's the ROI of that? I don't know, but these good people become our advocates of the brand forever. We are creating a sense of partnership, community, and collaboration, and I think it is invaluable. So these conversations around ROI and how much we should spend, they always come, but it is an ROI we can see with each person we are helping at a very critical moment."

When we talk with businesses about the idea of giving gifts, there is frequent pushback from those who don't consider their company or the products and services they offer appropriate for building fans in this way. For example, many people claim it is impossible to build a positive fan culture if the product or service is a commonly available product. Batteries are certainly such a product, and Duracell is creating fans for life by giving gifts at a time of need. How many friends, neighbors, relatives, doctors, coworkers, bus drivers, pharmacists, etc., did that woman tell over the next twenty-four hours or will tell in the next twenty-four years about her Duracell experience, and multiply the people those people told, and on and on. That's your ROI from saving one little boy's life.

For example, one person helped by PowerForward commented: "The storm has not been good, the house is cold, we're out of everything, and everywhere is closed or cash only. We'll make the best of it. And now we can use flashlights!" Somebody else said: "We appreciate that Duracell came to town with the truck and is giving us this relief."

Velutini says there are just two ways to do business with a commonly available product. "One is to be the low-cost provider and have the benefits of scale and you try to win the market just on price," he says. "But that's just one model and that doesn't work for us. We've done the extreme opposite. We have a brand that has been constructed for decades. We have great equity. We're constantly one of the most trusted brands in America. The only way forward for us is to continue expanding that and continue deepening the relationships with consumers and PowerForward is one of the ways we do it. We have other ways such as helping with hearing loss for communities and that has also built an emotional connection to our brand. When Warren Buffett purchased Duracell several years ago from P&G, he acknowledged the brand is the competitive advantage, or what he calls an 'economic moat' for the business. He knows how important the Duracell brand is for long-term sustainability. Anything we can do to strengthen the bond between consumers and the brand, so people always have you top of mind means you're going to win."

There is a recap of one of the PowerForward deployments on the Duracell YouTube channel. Dozens of people surrounding the Power-Forward truck are being given free batteries in the days after a devastating storm. Some of those people have lost their homes, but they are smiling and happy even though they are facing tough times. One man comments: "We see the name Duracell and we say, you know what, those are the people who helped me, so those are the ones I'm going to stay loyal to. The people who help you, the people around you, when somebody comes through for you, that's powerful."

As we were wrapping up our fascinating discussion, Velutini offered another observation that we hadn't considered. "This is not only great for consumers, it's also immensely popular and successful internally here at the company," he said. "There's a sense of purpose for what we do and why we do it. I think moments like those where we help people with PowerForward bring together our agencies, bring together our employees, and bring us closer to consumers, and I think the value of that is impossible to measure. What we had to do to get seven hundred thousand batteries shipped quickly to Puerto Rico is really hard to do, and it only works when you have a full team 100 percent on it. It's one of the programs that people talk about in the company parking lot. They have PowerForward stickers on their cars. We create that sense of pride internally, and that also pays like nothing else when we see first-hand how our program helps the lives of millions of people."

Charlie's Taxi: How One Man Can Compete with Uber

Gifts build fans and result in people sharing on social media and in person to their friends. A gift is often so unexpected that we can't help but feel compelled to talk about it.

When I needed to go from my hotel at Sydney Olympic Park to the international airport for a flight to Los Angeles, I asked a hotel staffer to call a taxi. About halfway through the forty-five-minute ride to the airport, my driver turned to me and handed me a pen with the words "HI CHARLIE" (in all capital letters) and his telephone number on it. I smiled and said, well, you know what I said. It's obvious, right? I said, "Hi, Charlie!"

At first, I thought I didn't really need a pen, and was about to give it back. And then I started to think about this gift. The hotel called Charlie's cab over the other cabs in the area, so he is doing something right to get that work. But with Uber and other ride-sharing companies, the traditional taxi business is getting squeezed. How can an independent taxi driver compete? The pen is an interesting way to stand out and be remembered.

And then Charlie gave me another unexpected gift.

When we were about a mile from the airport, Charlie did something I've never experienced before in hundreds of cab rides in cities all over the world. He turned the meter off at exactly one hundred dollars. We didn't set that as a fixed price, and I was happy to pay the full fare. He just turned off the meter!

At the end of the ride, I tried to give Charlie a tip, but he refused.

I had such a great experience, I shared it on my blog. And now I am sharing with you.

A few months later I was in Sydney again. This time, I didn't ask the hotel to call me a cab. And I didn't use Uber. This time when I was ready to go to the airport, I knew what to do.

And when I got into his cab for the second time, I greeted my driver with "Hi, Charlie!"

Just as the free pen had prompted me to do.

CHAPTER 7

Build Identity to Become More Than the Product

by Reiko

The very first friend I made in medical school was because of a sweatshirt.

It was friendship at first sight, as I spied the bold red and black from across the room. In a crowd of logoed T-shirts and colorful sweaters, it didn't look like anything too special on its own, but I recognized it immediately. I made my way through my new classmates and caught her eye.

"*Mass Effect*?" I said, pointing at the N7 stitched onto the front. It was from a role-playing shooter video game by BioWare where you play as a human commander of a spaceship, meeting aliens and saving the galaxy.

"Of course!" she said, her face slipping into a smile like we were old buddies. Like we already had inside jokes and could laugh as if we'd known each other for years.

Medical school orientation was stressful for me in many ways. Caught up in anxiety surrounding the upcoming academic rigor and responsibilities, I had almost forgotten how to make friends. Trying to look put together, intelligent, and competent, I stumbled over formal introductions and handshakes, as if I were being interviewed for a spot in this class.

Formal handshakes? That is *not* how I've ever made a friend before.

Lined up in our professional attire, suits and jackets and brilliantly white coats (that would not stay white for long), it was hard to distinguish one of us from another. Our outfits represented our profession rather than our personalities. I thought of them as coworkers or colleagues rather than friends.

That *Mass Effect* sweatshirt indicated something much more. It said she was a gamer, of course. But it also told me she liked stories—the same sort of stories I did. It told me we could have a conversation about these characters I loved, and I wouldn't be laughed at for liking something so much. That brand symbol went beyond video games to something deeper. Our identities.

More than anything, it was comforting to know I could walk up to her feeling like I already knew her on some level.

"You play too?" she asked me.

"I think I played through all three in about two months," I said.

"Nerd," she said with a smirk. The way she said it, though, made it sound like a compliment. "I'm Victoria, by the way. I think we're going to get along." She was right.

Coming of Age and Becoming Ageless

When I was young, through preschool and grade school, it was simple for me to flit from one activity to another. I could be an artist one hour, gluing paper cutouts and making sculptures out of sand, and an athlete the next, climbing the monkey bars and doing somersaults like a gymnast. Or I could be everything at once—an astronaut, a vet, a firefighter, a mermaid—because my friends and I didn't yet identify ourselves by what we did.

The world shifted as I got older, especially when puberty hit and the social pressures of school and home became more complex. What I did and what I loved became more than just activities. I didn't just swim after school, I *was* a swimmer. I didn't just like science, I was studying to *be* a scientist. What I did seemed to become viewed as an expression of who I was. I was now the adult identity I had been building.

Throughout human history, initiations or rites of passage both religious and secular have been commonplace during the teenage years. Many societies continue to practice formal rites of passage from childhood to the adult world, ritualized, codified, and practiced from generation to generation. Bar and bat mitzvahs in the Jewish tradition happen at thirteen and twelve, respectively; *Khatam Al Koran* in Malaysian culture at eleven; confirmation in the Catholic Church typically in the middle teenage years; the Latin American quinceañera for girls at fifteen; and Rumspringa for the Amish culture at around fifteen; to name a few. Even the American "sweet sixteen" and test to acquire a driver's license is like a ritual to re-create this journey to adulthood in a widely nonreligious community.

My father and I had an opportunity to learn about one such ceremony from Iniquilipi Chiari, president of the Guna Youth Congress, who is on staff with Panama's Ministry of the Environment, which specializes in indigenous affairs and protected areas. The Guna are the indigenous people of Panama and Colombia living today in an autonomous nation in the traditional ways they have for centuries. We met Chiari in the Guna village of Gan Igar, located on a hilltop overlooking the Cangandí River near where it flows into the Caribbean.

"When a girl becomes a woman, we have a ceremony called Iggo

Inna to present her to the village society," Chiari told us while we shared a meal of fish and bananas that had been cooked on an open fire in a bamboo and grass hut owned by a hunter and his wife. "At the ceremony, we give a traditional name signifying she is ready to get married."

Before the Iggo Inna coming-of-age ceremony upon reaching puberty, girls also go through a kind of baptism at around age four when they receive their first haircut, an occasion celebrated by all the people in the village. The Guna are a matriarchal people, and only girls go through these ceremonies.

"The coming-of-age ceremony lasts an entire day," Chiari says. "It takes place in the largest hut in the village. All the adult men in the village sit on one side and the adult women on the other. The master of the ceremony leads singing, dancing, and drinking of a rum-like traditional alcoholic beverage made in the village. The girl's body is painted with a seed that creates a dark blue color, and she is formally presented to the entire village."

According to Chiari, the ceremony is a joyous and fun occasion. "I love it. It's my culture. I hope it can last forever in the same way to conserve our identity as a Guna."

However, in the United States, Panama, and elsewhere, the initiation into adulthood is not only a structured, top-down phenomenon. The way older children and teenagers introduce themselves into adulthood, out of the spotlight and within their own time, is with their identity around the things they enjoy. Their fandoms. The graphics of rock bands they wear on their T-shirts, the makeup tutorials they choose to follow, or the online forums they join are all more than what they seem from the outside. Sometimes, an initiation rite can include an element of perceived danger such as a first LSD experience in hippie culture. They are today's modern, self-directed rites of passage. They are the way young people show us what sort of adults they are becoming.

In our research for this book, we asked several thousand people who identified a fandom they were involved with at what age they started to become interested in that subject. The median age of the responses was twelve years old.

> **Rites of passage we experience as young people profoundly influence the fanocracies we participate in as adults.**

Isn't it interesting that age twelve is also the same time we face new responsibilities and new challenges? Does that feel familiar? We develop new bodies and new hormones. Adversity seems to show up at that age more than it did before, in both what others expect of us and what we expect from ourselves. School, bullies, peer pressure, and friendships all suddenly seem so much bigger or more intense than we had previously faced. Consciously forming an identity was an answer to that because it offered us a source of stability in an otherwise intimidating world.

We build, piece by piece, our identities using both family tradition and pop culture references. And still, even after decades of identity building, those early steps into adulthood formed the basis of who we would become. Those brands and experiences stay with us.

MuggleNet: Where Harry Potter Fans Share

Emerson Spartz was twelve years old in 1999 when he founded Mug-gleNet. The early internet was his place for initiation, where building websites and sharing them with others was a way for him to explore his identity. Now MuggleNet is the most popular Harry Potter fan site in the world, but when he started, it was just a way for him to review other Harry Potter sites and meticulously collect facts and news that would only be of interest to other obsessive fans like him—things like listing every animal mentioned in the books or every proper noun used. Mug-gleNet remarkably cultivated a massive audience, with fifty million page views per month. Then, Spartz wrote a *New York Times* bestsell-ing book and hosted live events with tens of thousands of people in attendance. During the release of the sixth Harry Potter book in 2005, J. K. Rowling invited Spartz to her home in Scotland for an exclusive interview by him. Sick of being asked the same questions by the main-stream media, Rowling chose Spartz's voice to represent Harry Potter fandom.

Spartz is interested in fandom of all sorts and notices trends in a way few do. He studies the way fans post on forums such as Reddit. Some of the fandom posts include a picture of somebody with their first ever product and another fraction are of people who have reached a celebratory milestone, an achievement of some kind, like one year interacting with this topic. Spartz too pays close attention to these initiations, traditions, and values as a reflection of our culture's coming-of-age. "I think you can map out how fandoms work in the same context of these ancient traditions and rituals that also form the basis of religion," he says, adding, "It's the sort of social technology that we have, the bedrock of collaborative systems at work."

For Spartz, creating and managing MuggleNet was his vehicle into adulthood—into the fandom he'd be a part of his whole life, as well as his career. It was a way of taking something he *liked*, these books he'd read over and over again, and making it *his*. "When you passively read something, you're stepping into a universe that somebody else created. You're making a copy of yourself and that copy exists in the form of a character. You become Harry and you save the world," he told us. "But when you participate in the creation of the world, you are taking ownership of the idea, the content, yourself. Like in business, getting stock in a company creates ownership and thus makes people want to work harder to grow the value of the business. Participating in the creation of content around a world can make you feel like an owner."

> **When someone takes ownership of a brand they love, it becomes part of their identity.**

Spartz designed MuggleNet to become a fanocracy around this idea of self-expression he now sees as common in many fandoms—fans taking ownership of what they love and making it their own. "Our business model was to basically make it really, really easy for people to contribute," he explains, so that he could make other fans also feel like owners of their fandom. In the early days of the site, he put up pages that didn't yet exist of content he would like to see and wrote "email me if you're interested in helping" so *other* people could supply the content. Many people contributed occasionally, but some of those volunteers found their identity in being a big part of the content-creation work on the site. It became a way both for the website to grow and for the contributors to identify themselves as big fans and participate in the community. Spartz was able to help people ignite a spark in themselves simply by their participating in the creation of the content—this was a place where people who were also coming of age could find safety in this new identity.

"Once in a while you get a diamond in the rough—hardworking, passionate, and smart," Spartz says of the contributors to MuggleNet. "They end up taking on more and more responsibility and then you give them more opportunity. Then, they take on more responsibilities that they create themselves." For those who did the most for the site, it became part of their identity. MuggleNet continues to operate that way, designing the site and organizing the community in a way that will continually increase the number of people contributing.

After MuggleNet, Spartz went on to found a company called Dose, aimed at building a network of viral content websites, which has raised $35 million in capital using the same techniques as he did with the Harry Potter fandom.

"People often have an overly narrow definition of what it means to be a fan," Spartz says. "We need to think about a fan as a really happy customer, you have the beginning of a relationship." What you do with that relationship, such as what Spartz does by encouraging his customers to contribute, is what builds that relationship going forward, making those fans feel that this product or experience is part of their identity.

Air Jordans: A Different Kind of Status Symbol

"Teenagers and adolescents don't relate to businesses as much as they relate to the brands," says Juma Inniss, the director of the Message, an organization that helps teens to become empowered adults through workshops and inspirational talks. "When they relate or connect to a brand, it's a more profound connection in that at that life stage they're assembling and figuring out identity," Inniss says. He uses live music and popular culture to help young people gain literacy on current technology and use that knowledge to support them through their transition to the working world.

Inniss teaches through pop culture because he understands that people give emotional weight to decisions that are tied to their identity. To many young people, what bands they listen to, what clothing they wear, and what celebrities they follow on social networks are ways to show others who they are. Even the most mundane decisions about what products teens choose can be shaped by personal story.

One example Inniss shares is the Air Jordan sneaker made by Nike, a status symbol in both urban environments and more affluent communities, and the most influential sneaker ever made. It's just a shoe, many adults can argue. They don't understand the price tag associated with it or the hype around new releases. However, to young people growing up, it's much more than simply footwear.

It's not just a product when it becomes a status symbol.

"It's an iconic shoe," Inniss told us. "Since I was young, having a pair of Jordans was like, *whoa*. They've done a great job at remaining relevant and keeping their place in culture throughout time, in the past twenty to thirty years." For generations, young people have gravitated toward Jordans because they connect with the people they see wearing them.

At the start, it was Michael Jordan. "At the height of his career, everyone wanted to be like Mike," Inniss says. "He was a super-aspirational figure. Nike smartly priced his shoe out of the typical consumer's access point. Thinking about it, back then that was a bold move, but it paid dividends because a lot of urban kids thought if they can afford that, I'm doing well. I'm someone people should take notice of. Some of those kids went on to be amazingly successful. Today, Jordans' lead ambassador is DJ Khaled, who is perhaps the biggest influencer in the Gen Z space." The shoes have remained a status symbol because a new generation of idols, after growing up with the influence of Jordans, has made the brand their own.

> **Kids see themselves reflected in the brands they interact with, and those are the fandoms they stay loyal to as they grow up.**

"Some brands can indicate cool status, or counterculture status. Brands, whether they're technology, consumer, or retail, play a huge role in the adolescent life in that they are used to communicate identity—how they see themselves and their place in the world."

So what is the difference between a brand that is successful among Gen Z and one that fails? Inniss says it's about knowing that brands have a power to mean more and using that platform to their advantage. Especially in socially responsible ways. "There's a recent Nielsen survey where 72 percent of the teenage cohort said they were willing to pay more for products and services that were committed to positive social or environmental impact," Inniss says. "There's a sense of tightened social awareness that is undercurrent, that is a theme, to Generation Z."

How does this expand to all fanocracies? A shoe can become more than a shoe because it *means* something to the individual in their life outside the product. A certain product means that kids know what's cool or they follow or try to mirror certain celebrities. A shoe itself tells a story about the wearer. In the same way, many young people choose brands that are socially conscious because they know it will reflect back on them, as if to say, "*I* chose this brand because *I* want to be seen as caring about the environment." It carries weight in decision making because it reflects how these young people think of themselves and how they want to be seen by others.

Magic: The Gathering—An Old-School Card Game That Succeeds in Our Digital Age

Brands are not only powerful ways of identifying ourselves to others, they can also be how we explore who we are. A way not just to show, but to *create* stories about ourselves.

My husband, Ben, recently brought home a box filled with old playing cards he'd found in his parents' basement. They weren't the standard fifty-two-card deck with the traditional suits. These were rather fantastical, filled with drawings of elves and dragons and magicians, trampling dinosaurs and gruesome goblins. It was a fantasy card game Ben used to play when he was ten years old. The card game is called Magic: The Gathering, with play centered on a battle between opponents with decks, each player using "creature cards" (a vampire or a mermaid or a charging rhino) or "spells" to attack the other player, decreasing their life total. The winner is the last player standing with life.

We had always been a nerdy pair—we met in high school band—but this game seemed outside of our normal brand of geek. I was skeptical. But when I saw how excited Ben was about it, I knew this was something I needed to try. If only to celebrate something that made Ben so happy.

But after several how-to YouTube videos and referring to an instruction page open on my computer, I got used to the complex play.

And I got hooked.

What makes this card game special, and perhaps why it has sustained its popularity for more than twenty-five years, is that each player enjoys a unique experience in how they choose to play. With thousands of cards to pick from, and with new cards constantly being released, gameplay and strategy are always shifting. The game is individual to the player, as you can choose any combination of cards to fill your sixty-card deck. So someone like me, who enjoys playing defensively, will pick creatures and spells that will protect my life total from attacks. Someone like Ben, however, likes collecting cards with big creatures that can attack head-on, ramming through any defenses I might have put up and hoping he can kill me before I can retaliate. This single game can allow us to fit our individual strategies, our own narratives, and brings to life our personalities to each other, all at the same time.

Mark Rosewater, head game designer at Wizards of the Coast, the company that produces Magic: The Gathering, speaks a lot about the work that goes into making a game feel both expansive and intimate. Expansive because of the sheer number of cards in circulation, each with beautiful art, as well as a story line connecting the cards to a greater fantasy universe online, and intimate because of how easy it is to tailor the game to the individual.

"People place value on stories about themselves," Rosewater says in his podcast about making Magic: The Gathering. So Rosewater makes sure he designs the game with enough flexibility to allow for these personal stories. He wants players to use cards in ways he didn't think of when he was designing them. He purposely builds in elements that could be mixed and matched in individual decks to make for more interesting plays. By letting the personal story, the personal decision, matter, he makes it live in the real world.

When designing the game, Rosewater became aware of something surprising. He learned that players don't always choose strategies that will bring them to victory the fastest. Many times, they *go against* what is logically the best move to win the game because they see an opportunity for a better story to tell. For many players, winning wasn't as important as the sheer enjoyment of playing the game in an interesting and new way.

For another example of narrative sometimes being stronger than winning, consider the 2018 Major League Baseball World Series championships. It was the Boston Red Sox versus the Los Angeles Dodgers, and by game five of seven, the Red Sox needed to win only one more game to take the title. I overheard many die-hard Red Sox fans talking about how they'd actually *like for the Sox to lose* the next game in Los Angeles so that the home field would come back to Boston and the Sox would have two games in which to win the series on home ground. *They* wanted to be in the city where it happened. *They* wanted the experience, even if it meant losing game five. That feeling is the same as what Rosewater is going for, and what I experienced, in Magic: The Gathering.

The idea of personal narrative in a card game has made Magic: The

Gathering one of the most popular games of any kind currently made, growing quickly since the 1990s when my husband, Ben, first played. Yes, remarkably enough, a wildly popular physical card game is a true fanocracy in the age of high-tech video games! Now Magic: The Gathering has twenty million players worldwide, with tens of thousands of distinct cards in print, many rare ones prized by fans. Acquired by Hasbro in 1999 for $325 million, Magic: The Gathering continues to be one of the company's most important brands, earning about $250 million annually.

No matter how it manifests within a company or professional, what matters is understanding that stories have a value in themselves. What brands can learn from Rosewater's insight is that developing products that value flexibility—the capacity for each individual to take a mass-produced product and somehow make it their own—pays enormous dividends as those individuals continually invest in and trust the brand. They become fans because—even though the product is mass produced—they are able to assign emotional weight to decisions about how they use the product. Providing room for the individual to incorporate a product into their lives is a quality that will make it successful because people care about expressing themselves as individuals.

Ben and I keep coming back to Magic: The Gathering because it's a way for us to spend time together. I've learned things about him I wouldn't have before, like that these cards he treasured when he was young were some of the inspirations for the styles in which he drew as he grew up. The game was a window into his past and a way for my curiosity to have an outlet. It is more than just a game.

The household in which I was raised didn't do much in terms of religious rites, and I didn't have much of a sweet sixteen. I got a driver's license because I needed to drive to school, but I never liked driving. When I graduated from high school, I went straight to college. More school felt like the next step, the logical progression, rather than something that marked me as changed. There was no moment I could cling to as my moment to become "an adult."

What I do remember is the first concert my dad let me choose for myself—P!nk, when I was in elementary school. By the time I was in middle school, more than simply liking a band, I went out of my way to show off what I listened to. I was the kind of girl who was a fan of metal, and wore the T-shirts to prove it—HIM, Linkin Park, and Disturbed.

I remember defining myself by my favorite books, lugging around the volumes in public hoping someone would ask me about them. I remember the power in those Scholastic book drives, being able to pick your own books to take home. Then, at twenty-five years old, I manufactured my own rite of sorts to mark the impact a particular book had on my progression from childhood—a tattoo of two snakes in the form of an *ouroboros*, AURYN from *The Neverending Story*. More than fifteen years since I first read that book, it was continuing to shape me, both on my skin and in who I was.

Looking back, I can't disentangle who I am from the brands and titles that lead me from childhood to now. My adolescence didn't just involve the books on my shelf or the shows on the TV or the clothes in my closet, it *was* those things and more. I owned those things, identified so strongly with them, that I still wear them proudly on my body.

And now, still, I make friends with others who do the same.

Mass Effect—a single-player video game I mostly played alone on my couch—was able to bring Victoria and me together. The sweatshirt was more than a sweatshirt because our shared fandoms became the basis of our friendship. It's our shared experience. So the video game has become more than a brand—it's part of our identities.

CHAPTER 8

Be Smart About Influencers

by David

When KCDC Skateshop was brand new in 2001, the Brooklyn skateboarding scene was a counterculture haven for people following their own muse in a gritty part of New York City. This was during a time when most were simply worried about the future, because 9/11 was fresh in people's minds and the Twin Towers had just fallen a few short miles away in Manhattan. KCDC thrived by providing a place for people to hang out with those who shared the same passions.

Now, some two decades later, skateboarding has evolved into a lifestyle accessible to anyone who is interested. Manhattan has rebuilt, and Brooklyn is now one of the hippest places on the planet. At the same time, with online stores offering all the products required by skateboarders, a store like KCDC has to evolve, like the city of New York has done, in order to thrive.

"People in their thirties are having families and having kids," says Amy Gunther, owner of KCDC Skateshop. "It's the first time in skateboarding where your dad might have grown up skateboarding and your mom might have grown up skateboarding. But Dad can't go online to show their kids what it meant growing up with skateboarding in their lives: the music aspect and the community aspect and running into your friends. You don't run into your friends when you buy a pair of sale shoes online. A dad bringing in his son to show him the skateboards—that's the difference."

KCDC offers skateboards, skate gear, and lessons plus men's and women's apparel, and has become more than a resource for skateboarders. It's evolved into a clubhouse for all kinds of creative types with art shows, music events, meet-and-greets with professional skateboarders, and parties to promote up-and-coming artists and companies in the skate industry.

RVCA: How Advocates for a Clothing and Lifestyle Brand Influence Customers

"My work was part of an art installation at KCDC," Josh Harmony told us. He is a professional skateboarder, a musician, and a visual artist who is a member of the RVCA (pronounced Rew-ka) advocate program. California clothing company RVCA is a global lifestyle brand with a heritage in artist-driven apparel and accessories fueled by a culture of creativity. "RVCA takes someone like me who's creating new art and making culture and then sends me out as an advocate and a representative of the brand. At KCDC, we participated in an event where a band played, we gave out stickers, and people skateboarded on the ramp at the store. It's a win-win because my brand and my art get celebrated through RVCA. They have the resources to make an event like that happen and then in exchange RVCA benefits from the art that I'm making."

A successful professional skateboarder since the age of seventeen, Harmony has been showcased in some of the industry's biggest skateboarding videos and magazines, including multiple *Thrasher* covers. He's a self-taught musician and artist living in California who has several solo albums and performs with his band Freckles, and his music has been used in skate videos. Harmony's artwork has been shown at galleries around the world and has been used for skateboard graphics by some of the industry's most respected skate companies. At KCDC, Harmony brought nine of his colorful and whimsical oil-on-canvas paintings of beach scenes and birds, with the largest painting depicting one of the telescopes at the pier in Newport Beach, California.

"RVCA takes what people do, their gifts or talents, and then packages it into a brand that's approachable," Harmony says. "In this case, at KCDC, I'm one of the older pro skateboarders. I'm thirty-five, so it makes sense for me to go there and introduce art because the younger kids can see the possibilities of a different career."

The "V" and "A" in RVCA symbolize the balance of opposites and how they coexist as an organic fusion of art and commerce. The company partners with athletes and talented artistic people who, like Harmony, have multiple passions.

"I started riding for RVCA when the brand began," Harmony says. "As I grew as a skateboarder, my passion for music and art blossomed as well. And RVCA used those aspects of what I was creating to market their brand too. With the identity of lifestyle and surf and skate culture, RVCA selects people who are actually *of* the culture and part of it. They ask me to play music at parties or bring my art to events to embody the spirit of their brand. RVCA considers what the person's doing as interesting or cool and marketable because their unique kind of marketing recognizes a balance in opposites."

Many companies like RVCA work with outsiders who act as brand advocates as a way to influence customers. A brand advocate is somebody who is eager to share what they know about your company, its products and services. An enthusiastic brand advocate can be an employee (as we will discuss in detail in chapter 12), a customer, an industry expert, or a well-known public figure.

RVCA has an advocacy program, and they are always looking for exceptionally talented brand advocates like Harmony. They want advocates who appeal to diverse subcultures, especially those who do not limit themselves to one sport, passion, or pursuit. What makes RVCA advocates different from the typical paid celebrity endorsement is the RVCA advocate group actually spends time getting to know one another and engage with customers like at the KCDC event. Beside a financial benefit they are invested in the RVCA brand because it fits their lifestyle. It's interesting to note that RVCA advocates are not merely a one-off transaction—they are completely engaged over the long term.

Obviously, with all those advantages, becoming an advocate for RVCA is a coveted role and is very competitive. As a result, the company has the luxury of being able to curate the best team possible. The advocate relationship with RVCA is exclusive, meaning that the artist or athlete is exclusively committed to RVCA for the term of their agreement, although they may work with other companies outside the clothing business. The agreements are for a minimum of two years and in many cases extended for a longer period. As you can imagine, the process of finding the right advocates is quite extensive. It can take a year to vet. It's a very organic and slow process to be selected to be on the team; moreover, the current advocates have a say about whether a potential new advocate can be invited to join them.

Tyler Culbertson, head of social media at RVCA, explained it like this: "Typically, lifestyle and action sports companies are focused on, say, surfing or skateboarding, or something else. However, the balance of opposites runs through everything that RVCA does. Our advocates include a group of amazingly talented artists coupled with the world's best surfers, the world's best skateboarders, and world champion mixed martial arts fighters."

Some of the other people besides Harmony who serve as RVCA advocates include Andrew Reynolds, considered one of the most important and legendary skateboarders of all time; Bruce Irons, one of the top surfers in the world; Sage Erickson, a world champion surfer who competes on the World Surf League Women's Championship Tour; and B. J. Penn, who is considered one of the greatest MMA fighters of all time.

On the artist side, advocates include American street artist David Choe. In the early days of Facebook, CEO Mark Zuckerberg commissioned Choe to paint murals in the company's offices because Zuckerberg was a fan of Choe's work. Choe wisely chose to be paid in Facebook stock because upon the company's IPO in 2012, his shares were worth about $200 million! As of this writing the shares would be worth over a billion dollars, making his the most expensive art commission ever!

"We have this group of amazingly talented artists, surfers, and skateboarders and we throw them all together," Culbertson told us. "Typically, these worlds coming together are like oil and water but somehow RVCA can pull it all together, so it makes total sense. Also, many of our advocates bleed across different subcultures. They might be a pro surfer, but they are also musicians and painters and the same with the skaters, they're photographers and zine makers or curators of all different things."

By working with several dozen celebrities like these, RVCA is deeply immersed in the culture of these amazing athletes and artists. They might come from diverse backgrounds—different sports, subcultures, and parts of the world—yet the combined mix of skills and experiences is extraordinary and powerful.

By bringing together a variety of diverse and talented professionals, you create meaningful human connections, and those connections lead to a loyal fanocracy.

"Some brands put an emphasis on competing, but that's not what RVCA does," Culbertson says. "We're more interested in the artist or the athlete expressing themselves as best they can. Creating content is the number one thing they do to support RVCA. They're wearing the product when they're shooting photos and filming videos. We just want our advocates to do what they do best, pursuing their passions and what they are an expert at. And we just stand back and watch."

For many years, before social media, careers in surfing and skateboarding were built on videos. "Going back decades, the action sports industry was way ahead of the curve in content creation," Culbertson says. "Now surfing and skating are focused on social media. So our advocates keep their social media accounts active with new content, giving fans a look behind the scenes of their travel, surfer, skate, or their artist life to highlight the other great passions they're pursuing."

Culbertson runs the RVCA social media accounts, including the company's @RVCA Instagram with over six hundred thousand followers. He works closely with the advocates to curate the content they generate to share on the RVCA social feeds. Pushing out the kind of content that RVCA fans will enjoy takes a lot of thought and imagination. The added luxury of curating images and video created by each of the advocates on their own feeds brings him joy.

"Instagram works best with super short and snackable content," Culbertson says. "So we're constantly pushing out new photos and video to the fan base featuring our team riders. I create shows each day, so our fans can expect a particular style of content exclusive to our Instagram. They know they're getting an experience and know they'll see the content first, before it gets reposted everywhere. I'm keeping it fresh, highlighting our products, highlighting and celebrating our advocates."

By connecting fans of sports like skateboarding and surfing with the stars of those worlds, RVCA has created their own fanocracy. That some of the culture rubs off and develops fans of the clothing RVCA makes is an added bonus.

Brand Advocates Enjoy Spreading the Word About *Your* Brand

When customers have the opportunity to establish an emotional bond with others as a result of doing business with you, it sticks. They feel compelled to experience it again and tell others about the fantastic experience you gave them. Ultimately, this is what will inspire passion and build your own fanocracy.

The celebrity spokesperson concept has been around for decades in print and television advertising. For example, in the 1950s, before he entered politics and was elected governor of California and president of the United States, actor Ronald Reagan was for many years the host of General Electric Theater. It was a popular weekly TV show, and Reagan's star power helped GE to build fans for their products. People felt they could trust him, and sales of GE products enjoyed success as a result.

The intimacy of having Reagan in their family living room created a believability that lasted in the minds of millions of people for decades. Many think this helped propel him all the way to the White House.

Famous for Being Famous

The concept of what many are now calling "influencer marketing" has become a popular way to generate attention. That means identifying the people who have influence over the buyers of a particular type of product or service or who are popular with a particular group of people and build marketing programs that will attract them.

Social media has become a common way for fans to interact directly with industry experts, actors, musicians, writers, artists, or the athletes they follow. As you know, many companies invest a lot of money on celebrities who become paid spokespeople for their brand, frequently through posts by the celebrity on social media. With a contract and financial transaction, celebrities trade their fame to the company for compensation, free meals, hotel suites, travel expenses, and designer clothes and jewelry. With celebrity endorsements, the company is looking to build greater positive awareness for the products or services they produce. And do they? Not necessarily.

Having one of the Kardashians wear a piece of jewelry to an event once and posting a photo of the evening on social feeds might generate temporary attention. Yet it's unlikely to lead to sustained sales if the Kardashian wears your jewelry only once and isn't perceived as a true fan of the product.

Or consider Miquela Sousa, a "musician and change-seeker" with 1.6 million followers of her @lilmiquela Instagram feed, who is actually a computer-generated avatar. She is one of an increasing number of robot influencers showcasing products, including those from Calvin Klein, Dior, and Samsung. While the use of a Kardashian to promote your product isn't likely to bring long-term benefit, at least the Kardashians are real people.

> **The best people to champion your ideas or products are those who are the most believable.**

Influencer marketing can also go sour with an influencer who is out of control or doesn't have a clue about how to best represent your company. Be aware that any negativity associated with somebody you hire to represent you can harm your brand.

Nike: Controversy Sells. Or Does It?

In 2018, Nike stoked controversy with a new advertisement in the company's ongoing "Just Do It" campaign featuring Colin Kaepernick, the NFL quarterback who in 2016 chose not to stand for the playing of the national anthem to protest racial injustice. The choice of Kaepernick as a brand advocate was a gutsy move by Nike because of the controversy surrounding him.

In a postgame interview during the 2016 preseason, Kaepernick explained why he chose to protest: "I am not going to stand up to show pride in a flag for a country that oppresses black people and people of color. To me, this is bigger than football, and it would be selfish on my part to look the other way. There are bodies in the street and people getting paid leave and getting away with murder."

Immediately after Kaepernick's 2016 actions, his shirt became the top seller on the NFL website. At the same time, many people jumped onto social media to voice objections to what they saw as an unpatriotic move.

When Nike announced the relationship with Kaepernick, the hashtag #NikeBoycott began trending on social media. People shared videos lighting Nike shoes on fire. At the same time, thousands of people applauded the move and publicly supported Nike on social media.

There is always risk when a company chooses to wade into politics or take controversial positions. While 67 percent of consumers feel brands are credible when speaking out on social and political issues on social media, according to the *Championing Change in the Age of Social Media* report from Sprout Social, it's inevitable that some people will take offense and voice their displeasure in public. Yet the decision to use Kaepernick by Nike was bold and brash. It says a great deal about the Nike brand and generated a lot of attention. As a result, those who support Kaepernick are much more likely to continue to do business with Nike.

Generally, we suggest that companies be very careful about wading in with what can be seen as controversial positions on social issues. However, in a world where so much is increasingly polarizing, staking a claim like Nike has done shows what an organization stands for. It's gutsy and memorable.

Sarah Beth Yoga: Developing a True Brand Partnership

Because many celebrities take a fee to promote a product on a one-off basis on their social media feeds such as Instagram or YouTube, advertisers look to reach an audience through them. However, that's more like buying a single magazine advertisement than having that celebrity be an ambassador for a brand because they want to. These kinds of advertisements can result in people having a cynical view of you and what you offer because they see through the paid sponsorship posts.

"When I recognize a company and its products as something that I actually enjoy and use in my home, I'm much more likely to start a conversation," Sarah Beth told us. "The relationship is more important to me. It's more important that my audience trusts me, so when I do say I like a product, my audience will not think they're being pitched to because that's not at all my goal."

Sarah Beth is the creator and star of Sarah Beth Yoga, a free weekly yoga video series on YouTube with over 550,000 subscribers. She's also active on Facebook with 60,000 followers and on Instagram with 45,000 followers. Her yoga videos focus on stretching, strengthening, toning and de-stressing. In addition, she offers a membership plan and app for those who want a more personal approach to their yoga practice.

> **Your ideal brand ambassador has an authentic relationship with your company and is a true fan of the product.**

From the perspective of people who have potential to influence others, like Sarah Beth, the sheer volume of requests has become difficult to manage. Rather than build a relationship with potential brand advocates, the vast majority of brand marketers simply spam hundreds of people who have a following they want to tap, hoping that somebody will say yes to promoting their stuff.

"I receive more than fifty email requests a day from people who want me to promote their products," Sarah Beth says. "I can't even respond to them and I shouldn't because most of them are copy and paste email requests for me to review a product. It's obvious when they can't spell my name right and hard to decipher which of these offerings are even credible and which of them are things that are worth my time."

Sarah Beth has been working for several years with KiraGrace, a brand offering sophisticated athletic wear. "The relationship I have with KiraGrace is ideal, so we continue to work together," Sarah Beth says. "They send me an outfit each season and I'll wear it in my videos. I'm extremely selective now about the products that I will present. For example, I work with clothing companies I've developed relationships with if I feel very strongly that my audience would truly enjoy the quality of their products. Everything else that's a onetime product review? I'm not interested."

Reaching Business Influencers from Companies like Facebook, Google, Kraft, IBM, John Deere, and Boeing

The email to me from Lee Odden, CEO and cofounder of TopRank Marketing—a B2B marketing agency that works with companies including Adobe, LinkedIn, SAP, 3M, and Oracle—was simple, friendly, and warm: "When reviewing the B2BMX speaker list I was very happy to see you listed as a keynote speaker. I'm doing some promo of the event (as I am prone to do) and would love to feature you in an interview. Would you be game for that? If so, I'll follow up with details and promise to make it as easy and convenient as possible ☺."

I've enjoyed interesting conversations with Lee at marketing events and we are connected on social media, so I quickly agreed to help him. Lee explained he was creating an interactive guide about business-to-business marketing titled *How to Break Free of Boring B2B* to be published about a week before the B2B Marketing Exchange conference where some twelve hundred professionals gather to share ideas. In addition to me, Lee tapped about a dozen other experts to share their best B2B marketing advice, including Tim Washer, Pam Didner, Ardath Albee, and Brian Fanzo, who, like me, were all speakers at the event. Other people tapped to contribute to the report included B2B brand professionals from companies like 3M, Google, Demandbase, PTC, Fuze, Terminus, and CA Technologies.

The contributions were packaged in a fun and playful (certainly nonboring) interactive guide featuring an animated bear. The opening of the report reads: "B2B doesn't need to mean 'boring to boring,' yet much of business marketing has earned this reputation. In a world of information overload, buyers expect engaging content from sources they can trust." After I read the finished report, I shared on my social networks, tagging the conference hashtag #B2BMX and TopRank Marketing's Twitter ID, @TopRank. Many of the others who contributed to the report did the same, and together we reached many thousands of interested marketers. And a week later, many of us shared the ideas again while we were on-site at the B2BMX conference.

> **A brand advocate is a person who is eager
> to spread the word about something he
> or she cares deeply about.**

Odden and his team from TopRank Marketing had very cleverly tapped people to advocate for their company in a way that was beneficial to everyone involved:

- Each contributor, like me, shared what they knew to help create content that ultimately received wide exposure to marketers around the world.
- People attending the event as well as the wider community of B2B marketers could read what thoughtful people were saying about how to make marketing less boring and more compelling.
- The conference organizers got to enjoy the pre-event promotion.
- And all of the above contributes to more people learning about TopRank Marketing, the creator of the report.

"We are trying to attract and engage fans for our brand, and reports like this one are a big part of our approach," Odden told us. "We're looking to collaborate and cocreate content with experts who know this subject matter like the back of their hand. They can write in a few minutes and turn around to us what might take people less knowledgeable with less experience weeks or months to get back with us to share with audiences to create something of mutual value. Everybody wins. And events are a big part of this because it's a concentration of influencers all in one place."

How to Work with Brand Ambassadors

For brands to forge a true link between those who have built a following, such as authors, artists, and athletes, with those people's fans, they must learn how to form a deeper relationship between themselves and influencers, something that Odden pays attention to.

"Before a conference, we take the list of speakers and we load them into a software called Traackr, an influencer management platform," Odden says. "It crawls the social web looking for everything everyone's sharing and determines the topical relevance of those speakers based on keywords we enter. We can easily rank the speakers based on each person's audience, including who is most influential in our topics of interest. Then we consider those we know personally. It is a bit of art and a bit of science. From there, we invite people to collaborate with us on these reports."

Odden has been using this approach to work with advocates for seven years now, and it has proven to be a powerful way to build fans for everyone involved. He has worked with influencers at companies like Google, PayPal, PwC, Progressive, John Deere, Caterpillar, Kraft, Boeing, Intel, IBM, Marriott, Microsoft, Tumblr, and Facebook.

"We find people who have expertise in areas that align with how we want to be known," he says. "We want to create an opportunity to showcase their talent, to do something for them too. We do our best to create excitement for individuals who are influential and help to showcase and promote them. Many of those same people help us later."

About ten years ago, Odden created a list of the twenty-five most influential women in digital marketing, which generated great attention in the marketplace. He's updated that list annually. It's now called Women Who Rock Digital Marketing.

"Year after year, our community nominates new candidates for Women Who Rock Digital Marketing," Odden says. "This will be the tenth year and we are doing an event at the LinkedIn New York offices, inviting the women who rock to come and celebrate the amazing things they are doing in the digital marketing world. That event is a form of influence for our agency because we're recognizing and honoring women and their contributions in a genuine way. From a karmic standpoint, the return has been unbelievable. We don't expect it, yet the goodwill has been amazing. Many of the women on the Women Who Rock Digital Marketing list have talked us up to their networks and several have hired us to do marketing for their companies."

Odden has an authentic approach to cultivating relationships with advocates. "It's important to actually make the effort to empathize with your influencer, do some homework to find out what's important to *them*," he says. "Are they a book author or a keynote speaker and you can promote them in a personal way that's meaningful to them?

"But I would take a different approach with a person who represents a brand—they're influential not in a personal way, rather because of the brand they work for. It takes doing some homework and curiosity to find out what's important to each."

This approach to building fans has been an essential driver to the success of TopRank Marketing. "By being authentic and empathetic people care more about *your* success. They care about you as a *brand* and they care about you as a *person*. These credible individuals, at the top of their game in their industries, are opening up opportunities for us. In eighteen years of business, I've never needed to hire a salesperson, all our new business is from people coming to us."

Odden shared details with us about how a brand advocate program works in the business-to-business marketplace. Many of the same ideas apply in the consumer world. Cultivating advocates who truly want to support a brand because they like the company and its products and services is much more likely to build a fanocracy than merely paying for an endorsement.

McKinsey & Company: Tapping Alumni to Promote the Company

"McKinsey gave me hands-on insight on how to run a company," says Jørgen Vig Knudstorp, executive chairman of the board of the LEGO Brand Group. Knudstorp got his start in business working as an engagement manager at McKinsey & Company, a global management consulting firm, in its Copenhagen office. "I have an unending appetite for knowledge and learning. As a leader, I'm intrigued by knowledge. One of the great benefits I have as a McKinsey alum is knowledge resources."

Besides the current employees of an organization (which we will explore in chapter 12) and outsiders who become brand advocates, another very important group of ambassadors for a company is former employees, what McKinsey calls its alumni. These are people who worked at the company for a few years and moved on, some to go back to school, some to start their own companies, and some to work at other organizations. These people no longer work at the company yet still actively participate in the culture, and many, like Knudstorp, are passionate about it. When McKinsey alumni say positive things about the company, its products, and its people, it is an incredibly powerful endorsement.

McKinsey & Company has one of the biggest and oldest corporate alumni networks, with more than thirty thousand people who work in leadership roles across the private, public, and social sectors. They live and work in 125 countries around the world, with nearly twenty thousand outside North America. The company encourages these alumni ambassadors via the McKinsey Alumni Center website, the firm's official platform to help the global network of former consultants remain engaged with the firm, its knowledge, and one another. Every year tens of thousands of alumni and firm members engage and collaborate with each other in this dynamic network. Membership not only benefits former employees, it's also an outward manifestation of those employees' enthusiasm for having worked at McKinsey.

Focusing on lifelong career development and maintaining lasting relationships, the McKinsey alumni program unites key figures in the global business community. Like Knudstorp, many McKinsey alumni move into positions of great influence after they leave the firm. One in five McKinsey alumni have started their own firms, and 450 alumni lead enterprises over $1 billion. When those alumni talk up McKinsey, it leads to growing its fanocracy.

Experimenting with Chinese Internet Celebrity

"Near the end of my senior year of college, I gave myself a challenge: 'Could I become an internet celebrity in China?'" Stephen Turban, a mentee of mine and a recent graduate of Harvard College who is fluent in Mandarin, shared with us.

"I'd always been interested in the online fan culture in China," Turban says. "Young Chinese people spend dozens of hours each week following their favorite influencers. So I began to think, 'Could I be part of that wave?' My classmate at Harvard, Lara, was already a Chinese influencer. She and her twin sister, Sara, are internet celebrities in China with nearly a million followers on Weibo [a Chinese microblogging service similar to Twitter]. So, I asked her if she would be my *shifu*, my spiritual guide to internet stardom."

Turban downloaded the Weibo app and with the help of his *shifu*,

Lara, settled on a Weibo handle that roughly translated to "some guy named Stephen who goes to Harvard."

"I quickly realized I had only three marketable traits in China: I spoke Chinese, I went to Harvard, and my skin tone was roughly the color of skim milk. So, with a new title and a fully developed Weibo account, I was ready to begin my quest. I just needed to create content. Lara helped me construct a first post in Chinese with a quick joke and a picture of the two of us. After she posted it, she went back to her Weibo account and simply 'liked' my post."

And the floodgates opened.

Within minutes, Turban's follower count on Weibo went from ten to three hundred. By the end of the week, he had nearly seven hundred followers because a little bit of Lara's fame rubbed off on him. A simple like by her on Turban's post meant people wanted to know about some guy named Stephen who goes to Harvard.

Turban soon realized that his lack of any marketable skill could actually pay off if he started to create regular videos. He and Lara had an idea. "What if we filmed a video called *How This Foreigner Is Trying to Become an Internet Celebrity in China*?"

After a few hours of filming and editing, Turban's video was ready. He posted it on Weibo and waited. The video was a hit, and his follower count grew from seven hundred into the thousands.

He began posting on Weibo every day, frequently sharing photos. He also created at least one video a week and live broadcasted several times a month. Soon he had tens of thousands of Chinese followers and over ten million views of his videos.

"Learning to become an influencer in China was fun because of the people I met along the way," Turban says. "The most important group of people were my collaborators—Lara and several other Chinese influencers became some of my closest friends in college. The second group were people I'd call 'super fans,' people who followed my content religiously and who I became friends with virtually. For the most part, these were young Chinese students who wanted to learn about overseas education. We'd message every few days and I'd give them advice through personal messages, comments, and videos I'd create from their questions."

Turban enjoyed his journey to semifame in China, but after he graduated, he began decreasing his use of Chinese social media because he was questioning his motivations. "Am I seeking internet celebrity for the right reasons?" he wondered. "What did I actually want: Was it fame? Glory? A meme collection of my face comparable to Grumpy Cat? Over time, I realized that the parts I enjoyed, connecting with students and helping them through their problems, I could achieve without obsessing over the number of fans I had. So I began to slow down my social media posting and focus more on the relationships with fans and collaborators I had developed."

Several years after he graduated, Stephen Turban still occasionally uses Chinese social media. Unlike many people who have built large followings, he wasn't dependent on social media for income, so he never tried to monetize his status by taking sponsorship fees from brands. He has friends that he keeps in contact with on Chinese social media and still semiregularly posts pictures and videos of himself.

"Since I've ended my experiment to become a Chinese influencer, I've tried to keep the parts I like from Chinese social media (practicing Chinese, meeting real people, learning about pop culture in China) and get rid of the parts that I don't like (obsessing about the number of fans, likes, and comments)," he says. "Frankly, I'm grateful for Lara and for starting this journey of Chinese stardom. I learned firsthand about China, myself, and the wild world of social media fame. So I consider it a success."

CHAPTER 9

Break Down Barriers

by David

The elevator door opened, and Reiko, Yukari, and I caught a glimpse of several tables: white tablecloths, tall-stemmed wineglasses, gleaming silverware, each table with a single flower in a small vase. We heard laughter from guests farther inside for a moment, above the quiet music. The smell hit us: freshly baked bread, powerful and delicious. Hints of, what was that? Apricot, perhaps? Leather?

"Do you have a reservation?" the hostess said as we reached our turn at the front of the line of expectant diners.

I gave my name. "We booked the chef's table."

Her eyes lit up as she shared a secret smile with the three of us. "You're in for a treat."

We were escorted down a narrow corridor with countless bottles of wine on either side in floor-to-ceiling glass-enclosed storage units. Waiters and table bussers turned their backs to the glass, making room for us as we passed by. They each greeted us, sharing their happiness that we were the lucky ones that evening. A table waited just for us, the only one like it in the entire restaurant. As we entered the noisy, bright, and bustling heart of the restaurant, the smells from different prep stations competed for our attention. It was surprisingly loud, with sizzling and clanking, opening and closing. The action was framed by enormous gleaming stainless steel countertops and exhaust hoods. So much to see! But we'd have several hours to soak it all in. Nirvana!

All three of us were seated facing toward the big room, on a raised platform, our backs to a wall so we could see better. No menus were offered. Confidence!

The most expensive table at L'Espalier restaurant in Boston is also the one in the greatest demand. This table doesn't have the nicest view of some brilliant landscape, nor is it in a private room with a dedicated waitstaff.

It's in the kitchen.

Each evening, only one group of up to four guests sits at L'Espalier's chef's table, right in the thick of the action. During the fifteen-course meal selected by the chef as being among the best offerings of that particular night, the attentive staff explains not only the meal but also what is happening to prepare it. We learn what each food station is for and how the orders are handled.

At L'Espalier, we didn't merely enjoy an exquisitely prepared meal. We were a part of everything that surrounds it. We felt the heat from the gas grills as they seared the meat. We witnessed the occasional mistakes in dribbling a sauce just so and marveled as less than perfect food was sent to the trash. Some of Chef's assistants were working like crazy, juggling many different tasks, while others carefully, methodically performed the same action again and again.

What Reiko, Yukari, and I witnessed at L'Espalier that evening was way more than a wonderful meal. It was performance art that we will remember forever.

Beyond the Transaction

When organizations set out to provide a product or service, they typically make the crucial mistake of believing that they are only there to provide that product or service—as if they were merely there to fulfill a transaction. Is this the fastest, biggest, cheapest? Why should I buy your product instead of the other company's offering? Frequently, a focus on product attributes results in a race to the bottom with price discounts and shoddy service.

This is not a way to build a fanocracy.

Focus on product alone results in a race to the bottom.

In a world where breaking through the clutter of competitive offerings presents a challenge to organizations of all kinds, we see many attempts to stand out in the opposite way as well—not with discounts, but by offering extra perks, upgraded service, and enhanced products. But such approaches are usually just a bit of bling on top of a standard offering. These kinds of business models don't lead to creating fanocracies either. That's because typical consumers don't see the enhancement as something special or unique. Instead, they assume they are paying for the entire offering inclusive of the "extra." They see through the bribe. Been there, done that.

What was so special about the chef's table at L'Espalier is that it went beyond the simple transaction of eating at a restaurant. Being shown what's behind the curtain, being right there in the kitchen to witness the meals being prepared, made for a truly memorable experience.

Several years ago, free shipping of online purchases was unusual and generated attention from customers. No longer. Today even free overnight delivery is common, and when Amazon offers same-day shipping, getting your package tomorrow morning can sometimes seem quaint and outdated. Consumers don't see free expedited shipping as a valuable extra because they've learned to factor shipping into the total price they pay. Consumers are savvier than ever! And they have Siri and Alexa to help them all day long.

Consider for a minute the credit cards offered by airlines promising enough bonus points upon acceptance of an application and activating the card to earn two free round-trip tickets to Hawaii. Yawn. Yeah, whatever. What do the other airlines' credit cards offer? Can I get a better deal elsewhere? How about a pair of first-class tickets to New Zealand? *Anybody have that?*

Nordstrom, the North American department store chain, offers legendary customer service that is written about in books and taught at business schools. The most famous story about the company's customer service involves a man returning a set of four snow tires to a Nordstrom store and getting his money back. But, as you likely know, Nordstrom doesn't sell snow tires! That was more than forty years ago, and the story still makes the rounds and gets laughs. Yes, Nordstrom offers great service, but the merchandise offered in their high-end stores justifies the cost. When people choose to shop at Nordstrom, they already know they are paying a bit extra for excellent service. To customers, it has become a part of their business transaction. It's enjoyed yet expected.

In a world where thousands of brands advertise for our attention every day, we've become numb to the many offers presented to us. For the companies involved, breaking through is tough. While it's easy to get sucked into the arms race of more, faster, cheaper, and bigger, these commoditized approaches open us up to another company just a bit better.

At the same time, as we have discussed with hundreds of people around the world what makes them a fan of an organization, person, product, or service, what we hear again and again is that what makes it memorable is the *experience* offered. That's what we talk about and that's what we remember. That's what brings people together.

The opportunity to see how the food is prepared at L'Espalier made us fans of the restaurant. It wasn't just eating the food (although it certainly was delicious). *We became fans because we were exposed up close and personal to the process of how the food was prepared.*

Welcoming fans into our inner worlds melts barriers between seller and buyer.

When we are encouraged to peek behind the curtain to see for ourselves what's going on back there, when we even become part of what's going on once the curtain goes up, we're made to feel special.

And then we become fans. Forever.

IMPACT: Creating Emotional Context

IMPACT, an organization dedicated to helping people succeed with digital marketing, helps companies by developing marketing strategies and building websites, creating search engine optimization plans, and implementing social media marketing campaigns. Traditionally, a company like IMPACT would be considered a branding and design agency. However, founder and CEO Bob Ruffolo realized that to be truly successful, he needed to be more than a typical agency. Instead, he realized IMPACT needed to develop a fanocracy.

"We learned early on that people really look to us for insights into how sales and marketing can be done better," Ruffolo told us. "They want to know what's working right and what's not. They are eager to learn what's working with other clients and what they need to be aware of."

As a result, Ruffolo created IMPACT Live, a marketing conference, as a way to bring people together to share success and discuss the future of marketing. In 2018, the second year of the event, IMPACT Live brought five hundred participants together with the fifty-five employees of IMPACT and a roster of top speakers. Most participants are CEOs or owners of businesses or marketing and sales leaders in their companies.

The company devotes an entire year to planning IMPACT Live, and it is by far the biggest single initiative for the company. "This is like the Super Bowl of IMPACT every year," Ruffolo says. "Our employees are extremely proud to be standing there with clients and the interesting people who are speaking and thought leaders who are there, all under the IMPACT umbrella." The event also provides leadership opportunities for employees that go above and beyond their day-to-day job descriptions. Every employee has a job to do at IMPACT Live: they speak at the event, handle registration, work backstage, or manage relationships with sponsors and suppliers.

"We signed one of our biggest clients as a result of IMPACT Live in 2017," Ruffolo says. "She met the people who she would be working with on her account. She had worked with other agencies before but was impressed with actually meeting the team. As a result, she was able to make a much more informed buying decision because she got to experience us opposed to just the typical agency sales process. Meeting us face-to-face, she felt a lot more comfortable signing with us and here we are nearly a year later and she's a really happy client." In addition to signing new clients, IMPACT Live is important for maintaining relationships with existing clients. In fact, every client who attended IMPACT Live in 2017 was still a client a year later for the 2018 event.

What's significant about IMPACT Live isn't merely the commitment that Ruffolo and his team makes to the event each year, or the outcomes they enjoy, like signing new clients. We were amazed to learn they don't limit attendance! While many attendees at IMPACT Live are IMPACT clients, there are also a large number of people who are not. Anyone can attend, even people who work at other marketing agencies that compete with IMPACT for business. Who does that?

Maybe you've been to customer events hosted by business-to-business companies like IMPACT where the "enemy" isn't allowed. Where people who work for the competition can't get credentials to be admitted. That's the norm in the corporate world, right? Most executives would be very uncomfortable if their *competitors* were in the audience at their big meeting. We've all been taught in the business world not to reveal our secrets.

Despite the proprietary nature of the marketing strategies and tactics presented at IMPACT Live, the company operates counterintuitively. It is open and inclusive, and anyone who wants to attend is welcome. By offering seats to all comers, IMPACT brings people behind their curtain, sharing how they do business and what makes them special.

What is and is not a secret anyway?

It's unlikely that proprietary information at a closed event for five hundred people would not get revealed. *With the saturation and prolif-eration of knowledge, there are no secrets anymore—information can be found or leaked.*

"It's a big thing for our clients to come together at IMPACT Live and meet face-to-face with us and with one another," Ruffolo says. "It's much better than us visiting our clients by putting our people on air-planes and flying them all over. It makes our relationship with clients so much better and it turns clients into fans."

Few marketing agencies hold events like IMPACT Live. In my cor-porate career I've worked with probably twenty marketing agencies and none had in-person events like this. Creating an environment for clients to interact with one other and with agency employees and even with competing agency staffers is a great way to build your fanocracy. And it's also a wonderful way to grow business and maintain your cur-rent clients.

And there's another benefit. After experiencing IMPACT Live, some of those other agency people want to work at IMPACT. "After IMPACT Live in 2017, ten people who were there came to work at IM-PACT," Ruffolo says. "Some came on almost immediately because they were so impressed with what our company is doing, they wanted to come work with us."

While finding new employees is certainly an added outcome, the most important aspect of IMPACT Live is building a fanocracy. "Hav-ing fans is just so valuable for our business," Ruffolo says. "So I'm al-ways thinking about how we can find ways for people to love us more. I have a responsibility to bring our community together because they're clearly looking to us for that. IMPACT Live is our way of getting really close to our fans in an intimate environment and it shows social cred-ibility to future clients because we have this large audience and great speakers at our big event."

This closeness to fans is ultimately determined by the vulnerability IMPACT Live brings about—clients and competitors alike are shown some of the company's most cherished methods and ideas. By making themselves available to everyone in this way, IMPACT is demonstrating an investment in their attendees that then becomes reciprocated many times over.

When an organization creates this sort of intimacy, existing and potential customers (as well as competitors) relish their experience. There are many ways for you to create such experiences, which will form the crucial ingredient in your own fanocracy.

Grain Surfboards: A Business That Invites Customers into Their Inner Sanctum

Surfing is one of the most natural of athletic activities—it's you against the elements. The ocean is free for anybody who wants to jump in and catch some waves. The equipment is simple, a surfboard and, in colder climates, a wetsuit to stay warm.

For people who care about the environment, though, a standard surfboard has significant drawbacks. The first problem is the carbon footprint required to make the raw material—foam—then to ship the huge chunks of foam core to manufacturers, and then to ship the finished surfboards to distributors and retail stores. When the board breaks or reaches the end of its useful life, an old board is an enormous object to dispose of in landfills.

Surfers began seriously looking for alternatives to foam in the mid-2000s, at the same time that Mike LaVecchia founded Grain Surfboards, a company dedicated to building surfboards out of sustainable wood. The surfboards that originated in Hawaii over a hundred years ago were made from wood. However, they were made from one large plank and were incredibly heavy. They were long and wide in order to hold a person and, as such, they were difficult to maneuver in the water. LaVecchia pioneered the use of traditional boatbuilding techniques with ribs and planks to make hollow wooden surfboards. This innovation was exactly what was needed to give wooden boards the lightness and ability to turn that foam models have. The custom-built boards cost between $1,900 and $2,500, more money than factory-built foam boards.

The company goes one step further with sustainable techniques, offering a limited-edition Glenmorangie Original surfboard using repurposed surplus whisky casks from the Glenmorangie Distillery in Scotland. The crew at Grain Surfboards creates the interior framework that defines the shape of the seven-foot surfboard model from oak staves from used whisky barrels, replacing the marine plywood that is commonly used, a fantastic form of recycling.

"For the first year or a year and a half we were just making boards and we were trying to figure out how to do it, what the techniques were that we wanted to use so we were trying lots of different things," LaVecchia told us. "We quickly decided that it made sense to offer boards in other formats because it's expensive for customers to buy a custom board."

Initially, LaVecchia offered a kit so that people could make their own boards at home. By giving people all of the materials, plans, and detailed directions, Grain Surfboards was essentially inviting people to copy their proprietary surfboard-building techniques. The vast majority of companies protect their intellectual property, yet LaVecchia thought it would, in fact, help their surfboards gain popularity.

"We really enjoyed putting together kits and getting them out there," LaVecchia says. "Our whole thing has always been the more wooden boards the better, no matter how you do it. Wood is a great alternative to foam, and we want to help people use it. So it didn't matter if we built the board or if our customer built it. We're about getting wooden boards out there and proving to people that they are viable."

This is similar to the openness offered by L'Espalier restaurant through their table in the kitchen and to IMPACT inviting anyone who wants to come to attend their conference. Grain Surfboards packaged up their secrets in the form of a kit with detailed directions. However, there's more to how Grain Surfboards invited customers to participate in the creation of their own surfboards as they discovered another untapped market.

LaVecchia and the team at Grain Surfboards were getting inquiries from people who liked the idea of making their own wooden surfboard but didn't have the proper tools or woodworking experience. "There was a growing number of homebuilders that were a bit scared of diving into a kit project at home," he says. "The people who were confident had already bought a kit from us and were building, yet there were a whole lot of people who just needed a little help." That's when the Grain Surfboards four-day workshop was born!

Wooden surfboard enthusiasts come into the shop in York, Maine, to work side by side with the company's artisans to build a board of their own. Regularly scheduled classes at the factory are held once per month for up to eight students, and they add additional classes as needed. They also have a traveling class on the West Coast that stops near surf spots in California and Oregon and have a satellite workshop in Amagansett, New York.

I've gone through the experience at the Maine factory . . . *twice*! I loved it so much the first time that I came back to build a second board. Planning the board down to every detail is something I enjoyed. That includes personalizing my boards with a "logo"—the same red star tattoo I sport on my ankle is embedded into my two finished surf-boards. There's a lot of shaping work with knives and sanding to get the finish right. I found using a different part of my brain than I nor-mally do invigorating.

What I loved the most was interacting with the team from Grain Surfboards as well as the other students. We met in the mornings around a big communal table and ate breakfast together. From our whiteboard talk we'd learn what we were to accomplish that day, and we'd all be eager to get to work. The Grain Surfboards staff is there to help as much or as little as you need. They jump in to help you with the more delicate parts of the project, such as properly aligning the top of the board to the bottom ("closing the coffin" in Grainspeak). Over lunch and at the end of the day, sharing a beer or two, we talked (or told tall tales) about our surfing adventures. At my first class, I participated with a father and his twelve-year-old daughter who made a longboard together and a young man who had traveled all the way from India to make a shortboard. Little things like that bonded us students to Grain Surfboards staffers in a personal and powerful way.

"There's a lot of small steps and when you're first getting used to tools, there's room for error," LaVecchia says. "The closer you get to the finished product the more dialed in you're getting with all your tools. It's a rewarding process in that way. I think our students really enjoy working with us. For four days it's like they're part of our crew. They're using all the same tools we're using. If we're working on some custom boards, the students can see what we're doing, so everybody gets im-mersed in the culture here."

An added benefit of the factory location in York, Maine, is being within walking distance of Long Sands Beach. So if surf is up, students and crew can go out into the waves together. There are loaner boards available for students to try, which is how I ended up wanting to return to build a second board. I tried out the Paipo model, loved it, and wanted to make my own.

"I always joke that classes are great because it gives us a monthly excuse to stop and clean the shop to make it presentable," LaVecchia says. "Funny, yet it's honestly something we really love and look forward to, having people here. It brings new life here. Anytime we do a class it gets us excited to meet all these people. We just had a call ten minutes ago from a guy who has been coming here for the last year to visit and trying to schedule a class. But life was busy for him. He's a fireman and it took him a solid year to actually get here. He finally came in April to build a board and he just called to check in. Now we know his daughter—she went to school in Boston and now she's moving home. It's like they're all just now part of the family. Everybody who comes here somehow feels like they never really leave. Whether they come back to visit, or they just call to check in or post some photos of their board on social media. We truly value and enjoy getting to know all these people, it feels like we have this constant growing family."

And I can confirm that from the other side, it feels like I'm part of the family too. Remember from the opening of the book, those stickers I wrote about on my computer? How I showcase what I love and how I bonded with Brian Halligan because of my Grateful Dead, Japan, and Nantucket stickers? Well, one of my favorite stickers on my computer is the one from Grain Surfboards. I am a loyal and enthusiastic fan!

Grain Surfboards has built a fanocracy around their company that simply wouldn't have been possible had they stuck to just the transaction of selling wooden boards and shipping them to customers and dealers. People like me share our passion for the boards that we make ourselves by posting on social media, especially Instagram, which further fuels interest in the custom board-building experience. The @grainsurfboards Instagram feed showcases boards, classes, and surfing and as I write this has more than fifty thousand followers.

Giving people a chance to experience what most don't see is good business. As another example, the Stars on Ice shows offer skater meet-and-greets after every performance. For an extra one hundred dollars per person, fans can meet and mingle backstage with the stars from the show, including world champion Nathan Chen, Olympic medalists Maia and Alex Shibutani, United States champion Adam Rippon, and many others. Fans enjoy collecting autographs and bring cameras for photo opportunities. They share their experience on social media with their friends, which entices others to do the same.

Or consider how the German car company Audi invites its North American customers to travel to a European factory to get a tour, visit the Audi museum, meet the people who built their car, and take delivery of their vehicle there. They then have a chance to first drive their new car in Europe before it is shipped home. The company handles all the details including a pickup from the airport, first night's hotel, and the paperwork and logistics to get the car home after the journey.

Treating your fans as part of a family leads to your fanocracy.

The power of providing fans something special can move an organization from simply selling, to forging the memorable experiences that last a lifetime.

Coldplay: Creating a Bigger Fan Base
by Bringing People Together

So far in this chapter we've looked at such examples as a restaurant with a chef's table situated in the kitchen, Stars on Ice meet-and-greets with famous skaters, the ability to take delivery of a new Audi at the factory where it was built, and a four-day make-your-own-wooden-surfboard experience. Each of these outfits created fanocracies by connecting fans directly to the organizations that create what they love.

So how can artists and companies that serve huge numbers of people, where it's impossible for people to participate this way, allow fans to be a part of the creation process? It turns out that technology can play a huge role in bringing fans closer to artists.

Consider the British rock band Coldplay and their use of LED wristbands at their shows. Upon entry to the venue, each fan is handed a Xylobands wristband, a radio-controlled system that's run by the band's production crew. Multiple flash patterns are programmed on the full-color LEDs on every audience member's wristband to create a light show that every fan is a part of. Fans love them because the audience comes together as one with the artist to create a single, flashing, colorful organism.

Similar effects can be programmed to work on smartphones that people can hold in the air to be part of a show, a technology used by American electronic musician Dan Deacon. While the smartphone technology Deacon uses is less expensive than Coldplay's purchase of tens of thousands of wristbands for each show, fans must download the app ahead of time to be a part of the fun.

It's particularly fitting for Deacon because he is renowned by fans for his live shows. Reiko and I attended a Deacon show at Lollapalooza in Chicago a few years ago where he had nearly the entire audience throwing empty water bottles in the air at particular times, making fans a major element of the performance. Even though we saw a few dozen acts that weekend, one of the most memorable for us was Deacon's because he had us participating in creating the fun. We were an active part of the show!

During Coldplay's famous anthem "Yellow," everyone's wristbands light up, you guessed it, yellow! Most of the time the wristbands are dark, but during peak moments in the show, such as in the middle of "Charlie Brown," lead singer Chris Martin tells fans, "Put your hands in the air!" and a stadium full of wrists sync to the song he's singing.

Just like the way a handful of customers come together for four days to build wooden surfboards, tens of thousands of Coldplay fans come together for a few hours, and the wristbands make everybody a part of the show. When people participate in this way, the bonds create a fanocracy.

"Coldplay showed me how important the fan experience is, it's fan to fan," Nate Tepper told us. Tepper is the CEO and cofounder of Harmony, an app that empowers fans to vote on songs they want to hear at upcoming concerts. "In a sea of seventy thousand people, everyone is lighting up the same color at the same beat and I've never felt more connected to seventy thousand people. It was emotional and powerful to be one with the band and the music. I didn't even need to look at the band onstage to feel that. It's cooler to look at the lights because each light is another human being."

Harmony: Letting Fans Influence Their Favorite Music Artists' Performances

Tepper, like us, is a live music enthusiast, and he's turned his passion into a business. In 2015 Tepper and his friends traveled two hours to the Shoreline Amphitheater near San Francisco to see Dave Matthews Band. It was Tepper's third concert that week. He had also seen Trevor Hall and Counting Crows, but he was dissatisfied with all three. "Each of the concerts I'd traveled a good distance for, and I was so excited to hear specific songs," he says. "When they didn't play what I wanted to hear, I left feeling disappointed. Hearing your favorite song live is a simple way to create a better concert experience."

Tepper decided right then to solve the favorite song problem, so he created Harmony. Hundreds of artists, including Taylor Swift, U2, Ed Sheeran, Beyoncé, Muse, Tim McGraw, and Matchbox Twenty, use Harmony to communicate directly with fans. Harmony has a partnership with Ticketmaster where fans who purchase tickets are emailed a link to help create a set list, and then the bands share the link through social networks including Facebook and Instagram. Fans are taken to a unique Harmony page for each show and can vote on what songs should be played.

Fans can also upvote their favorite songs for a small fee, and the money from each vote goes to charities supporting homelessness, autism, suicide prevention, and cancer research. The more fans vote, the better the chance the artist will play their requested songs and the bigger the social impact. Some people vote dozens or in a few cases hundreds of times, yet fans only pay if the artist plays their chosen song.

The song request concept links fans to artists. When fans are empowered by influencing the set list, they take part in developing the show and feel a personal connection with the artist that they don't otherwise have. Fans take the time preshow to choose songs, and when an artist actually does play that song the fan chose, it gives a powerful jolt at the concert. The fan thinks, *I did this. I helped make that song happen!* That's especially true when the artist thanks fans for voting, as some do from the stage.

"We survey fans after shows and they tell us that when the artist plays their favorite song, they feel like they were a part of creating the experience," Tepper says. "It's amazing for them, like a direct line to the artist where you can influence the set list and the artist listens. Some fans tell us stories of why a song means so much to them and how they ended up getting to that show. It might be a couple and it's their wedding song. When the artist actually plays the song that they wanted to hear it's a moment of pure joy, a true moment of connection between an artist and a fan."

Artists love Harmony too, because when somebody uses the app to select an artist's song, that person's email address is shared with the artist so they can include it in their mailing list and connect more closely with fans. That's important because the ticketing companies don't share fan contact information with artists.

As I was writing this, I received an email from Ticketmaster with the subject line "What If Jack White Played All Your Favorite Songs?" The email was from Ticketmaster based on my purchase of Jack White tickets, and the link pointed to the Harmony app.

Create Your Dream Jack White Set List

We hope you're just as excited as we are about Jack White's upcoming tour! Get ready for your show by customizing

*your dream Jack White set list including songs from his
brand-new album* Boarding House Reach.

*Simply choose your favorite tracks, download your
playlist, and share with your friends!*

I chose a few songs including "Lazaretto," "Temporary Ground," and "Sixteen Saltines" for Jack White to play. A week or so later I was at the show. I was excited when White and his band kicked into "Lazaretto" as the second song of the show and later on played "Sixteen Saltines." Just by choosing the songs on the Harmony app, I felt more connected to White. It made me feel a little bit like an insider, even though thousands of others might have selected the same songs! Ha! Feelings trump reality every time!

Most big artists don't do their own social media today. Sure, there are some exceptions, but we've gotten to a point where social media is frequently run by a digital marketer behind the scenes. And it's not authentic or personal. It's usually just tour dates, ticket promotions, and merchandise offers. Some artists, especially more scrappy ones with smaller followings, are actually in control of their social media. They're getting more likes on their posts and more engagement, and those artists enjoy a good career because they can make a living from a die-hard fan base that goes to their shows.

"Authenticity is important," Tepper says. "Is it really your voice? Are you connecting to the fan? Or are you just telling them to buy tickets again and again. And that's kind of nice about Harmony. It's a real authentic connection where die-hard fans, like me, feel their voice is heard when they request songs."

The Rattle: Tearing Down Barriers
in Music and Technology

Sometimes the key to building a fanocracy is to actually build a business from the ground up, one that purposefully pulls people together in ways that have never been considered before. That's exactly what Chris Howard did when he founded the Rattle, a global community of facilities that offer studios, workspaces, and mentorship programs to help makers of art, technology, and culture thrive. In Howard's eclectic career he has been both a music producer and a technology company founder, so his insight was to bring the best of those communities together.

The Rattle brings together two wildly diverse groups of people— professional musicians and technology entrepreneurs—so that each group is exposed to the inner workings of the other. The cross-pollination of ideas sparks collaborations that are impossible in the environment in which a musician traditionally works—a studio with other musicians.

The typical early stage technology company begins its life in a technology incubator or coworking space. The Rattle is a mash-up of the two, providing a work environment for both the musician and the technology entrepreneur. However, the twist is they work side by side and feed off each other. Rather than providing insight into how a company creates its products, like Grain Surfboards, Audi, and L'Espalier restaurant, Howard exposes his customers to creative people outside of their typical sphere. The mixture proves electric!

Monthly membership to the Rattle includes free access to state-of-the-art music studios, engineers, producers, maker spaces, coworking spaces, mentoring, workshops, events, one-on-one coaching, and much more in several locations around the world.

The Rattle has developed a fanocracy of people from varied backgrounds and with different goals but who work together beautifully. "Tech entrepreneurs are showing the artists that their song is *not* the only way to make money," Howard told us. "In tech startups there are many ways to bring in money and in order to thrive those companies need to tap multiple sources. They're teaching artists that behavior to help them with what we call their side hustles, like performing in people's houses, which is really cool. Collaboration is genuinely happening every single day."

Fanocracy brings like-minded people together to celebrate what they love.

The Rattle's music-industry members range from independent artists turning pro who require recording time, mentorship, and business development assistance to small music labels and music management teams with a handful of artists on their roster. Many use the Rattle because they aren't ready to lease their own space. On the technology company side, members include startup founders looking for a place to base themselves and receive top-tier mentorship and a network of other entrepreneurs. There are also growing companies who want to be surrounded by top artists for the intellectual stimulation.

"Makers tend to respect other makers, so we put music artists and technology entrepreneurs under the same roof," Howard says. "There is a certain mind-set that is habitual for people who make technology and want it to thrive. We call it startup culture. That natural behavior is accepted in people who make technology, but you never really get into that if you are an artist. So putting people together means that the startup mentality can get under the skin of music artists because these entrepreneurial tactics can help artists to thrive. At the same time, we think we're significantly ahead of the curve in our philosophy of how entrepreneurship thrives in a creative world. It works both ways."

When an artist or band or indie record label joins the Rattle, Howard immediately sits them down with the entrepreneur in residence at that location. The artists typically only think about the traditional music route of getting signed by a major label. However, there are so many other ways to make a living in music, so mentorship helps them think through various options. This cross-pollination is something artists never receive when they work in traditional music studios, so the Rattle develops a founder mentality in music artists.

"At first, artists come in for about ten hours a week to rehearse or record," Howard says. "Soon they become addicted to the concept of empowerment and entrepreneurship and they start to come in much more regularly. They love to sit with tech entrepreneurs and have discussions and learn about business. They form bonds because of this superclose proximity. And it's really fascinating to see because before you know it, they're coming in every day and say it's like a holiday and they tell us it would be sad if they discontinued membership and they left. We've only had two people leave the cohort. It's astonishing how powerful it is to create unexpected bonds between people. And each side thinks the other side is cool! That's amazing!"

I've worked in several technology startups as an employee and over a dozen as an adviser, and I've witnessed the danger of getting into a formulaic approach to building a business. The artist members of the Rattle add a degree of creativity to their work that is impossible to get in technology incubators. I wish I had worked in such an environment. Well, maybe not, because I'd probably still be there, instead of writing this book!

"To be a creative entrepreneur you need to do something fundamentally remarkable, and you can't accelerate the company until that remarkable aspect is discovered," Howard says. "Tech entrepreneurs come to us to find what's remarkable about what they do and make it shine. Because they're together with artists, they get to test, iterate, pivot, and design in a way they never could in a traditional space and that makes them stick with us even when they get a little bigger."

Howard and his partners hang around the Rattle's locations whenever they are near. Howard deliberately schedules his time to be at the London location near his home all day on Tuesdays, Wednesdays, and Sundays and is available to take meetings with members.

The bond between members, especially the unexpected chemistry between wildly different people means the Rattle is a fanocracy in action. The humanity that develops when, for example, the musicians in a punk band hang out with a team of entrepreneurs building smartphone apps is powerful indeed. And these sorts of collaborations happen every day at the Rattle.

"We had an open house in London recently where members could bring friends or colleagues into the Rattle," Howard says. "And members were walking around with such pride, showing off the space, *their space*. And that pride resulted in many new applications for membership. People genuinely feel they are an early part of a movement and this is something they can talk about when they get older. Instilling a pride in the movement is a really important part of building our community."

When one of my handmade Grain Surfboards appears on the beach or in the lineup waiting for a wave, other surfers immediately notice the unusual wooden surfboard in a sea of typical form models. "Wow!" they say to me. "Cool wooden board!"

Saying I made the surfboard myself always gets people to stop and want to chat. "You *made* it?" That's my opening to share the story about my surfboard-making lessons at Grain Surfboards, while pointing at the company name burned into the wood with a hot branding iron. They love hearing about the class, including how I chose the type of board, selected the wood, learned to use the tools, and put in the work to build it myself. While the beautiful board generates attention, my enthusiasm for the process is what gets others really interested. My passion shines through, and people always want to know more: "Where is this place?" "How many other people are there?" "How long does it take?" "Is it difficult?" "Is it expensive?" What fun!

At a surf spot I frequent on Nantucket, people recognize my board more often than they recognize me! "Here comes wooden surfboard dude!"

Grain Surfboards found tremendous success by bringing fans into its workshop. The company discovered that including customers in the creation of their own surfboards serves as a bond between them and the artisans at Grain Surfboards. Making fans a part of the action at Grain Surfboards has been great for its business. It has built a passionate international fanocracy of people who are eager to be a part of what the company does. Those fans, like me, share their experiences on social media. And on the beach.

A great way to create love for what you do is to figure out ways to let people into your world. Allow them to create their own experience or be an important part of what you do. While everyone else is making products and services sold via transactions, *you create fans*!

CHAPTER 10

Listen to Rehumanize

by Reiko

During my time as an undergraduate working with my mentor, oncologist Dr. Raza, I had an experience working with a patient who forever altered the way I think about what doctors are meant to do. For the purposes of this story, I'll call him Henry. He had been diagnosed with myelodysplastic syndrome (MDS), a disease of the blood that drained his energy and left him perpetually tired. I met with him in the small clinic room before his appointment, and as we waited for his oncologist to come, he scrolled through his iPad to show me picture after picture of organic and twisting layered color. His art.

While Henry was talking about his art, it was as if the debilitating disease he was dealing with fell from his mind. I asked him how he made his work. He instantly became animated as he said, "I find interesting pieces of wood, small things people leave behind, and I arrange them like this in my studio." I lingered on one fascinating piece— wood, metal, and animal bones shaped effortlessly into the figure of a man grasping for something just beyond his reach. After explaining the origin of each element, he confessed that after he had gotten sick, it became too hard for him to go outside to find new materials and much too strenuous to cut and fasten them together. It was only since the care he received from this clinic that he was able to return to his long-ignored studio. "I finally feel like myself again," Henry said and laughed with a strong voice that surprised me coming from his thinning frame.

Looking from Henry back to the figure, I said that I enjoyed making art too, only my passion was writing rather than sculpture—creating from pixels on the computer rather than from wood and bone. He flashed a knowing smile and said, "Oh, good, you must know what that itch feels like. Only artists know the feeling of what it is like to *need* to make art."

The drugs that had relieved his anemia now allowed him to continue working in his studio, but he refused to go on harsher chemotherapy if it meant he would be too weak to make his art. That was the metric for his medical decisions: "Will I be well enough to be creative?"

He attributed his renewed confidence to the freedom he now felt to openly discuss his goals and fears with his oncologist. A doctor, who, like me, knew what it meant to be an artist, and what it meant for Henry to be in his studio.

When presented with the risk of MDS transforming into acute myeloid leukemia, he told me clearly, "I am not afraid of death. I would rather live a comfortable, productive life than be in pain. I refuse to be cooked on a spit before I die."

Up until this moment, like many students studying the sciences, I had assumed that human lives were counted in heartbeats, and the doctor's concern lay purely in the biological processes. The contemporary language surrounding death and illness often forces us to believe that life itself—rather than happiness, love, creativity, or independence—is what we are preserving when we attempt to help the sick. The biological functioning of the body and the label "alive" take precedence over other factors because of an often-prevailing attitude in science that "we can fix that." It can feel as though restoring healthy cells and blood and breath were the objective, because we can predict success in numbers of years.

Henry helped me realize that these notions I held were not enough for me to become the kind of doctor I want to be.

The decisions Henry was making held incredible weight. They were about life or death, comfort or pain. Henry helped me realize a doctor's responsibility includes sensitivity to each individual's needs, because the doctor's goals and a patient's goals are not always the same.

Before I left his room, Henry stopped me and said, "Doctors should be people, not robots. Remember that when you become a doctor."

The Alienation of Misdiagnosis

As a patient, Henry came to his oncologist for answers. He invested trust in her to help him make a decision that would alter the rest of his life. The interaction between him and his doctor, or even me as a student, already held emotional significance because here we were, after all, in a hospital room, talking about his future. However, it was our ability to be curious and listen to Henry about the details of his life outside the health-care system and outside the illness that gave him hope.

When our exchange with Henry took a narrative direction, meaning we were talking *with* each other, rather than to each other, it became an effective conversation. A different doctor might have insisted he undergo a harsher chemo treatment. "Wouldn't you like to live longer?" they might say, without completely listening to his answer. They'd have all the research data at their fingertips, despite the fact that it wouldn't feel right to Henry, who, if someone told him, "You have a 30 percent chance to live another two years," would feel unheard and not understood.

As a medical student I've witnessed this sort of contrast many times, such as the dramatic difference between the quiet conversations like the one I had with Henry and the harsh realities of what so many medical professionals do to help patients heal. We wait behind computers for test results to be presented to us. We calculate risks and benefits through apps on our phone.

I've had moments where I felt I was living a science-fictional future depicted in the novels I grew up with, for instance, when I watched a surgical robot dig deep into a patient's abdomen or saw a CyberKnife deliver focused radiation straight to a patient's brain. It's easy to forget that the unconscious body on the surgical table has a personality, likes and dislikes, personal pursuits and interests, family, loved ones, or a newborn at home, a job—a complete life outside the operating room.

In his 1963 book *The Birth of the Clinic*, French philosopher and social theorist Michel Foucault wrote about the "medical gaze": the separation between a patient's mind and body that occurs in the mind of the physician. As technology grew more precise, Foucault says that doctors became more drawn to lab numbers and biological signs and symptoms over the suffering person, reducing the patient from a complex human in sociological context to a single diagnostic condition.

We all do this at one time or another—dissect, judge, and tag the people with whom we work or meet for the first time. We divide people into pieces and use those to signify the whole.

"Illness scripts," or common presentations of common diagnoses, are a quick way for doctors to understand and treat conditions. They are powerful tools, and necessary for everyday care, but must also be used with the knowledge that they cannot replace the individual experience of each patient. With patients, we slip into easier language, calling someone "the diabetic" or "the trauma case." It isn't always because we don't care. Often, it is because we are busy and have so much on our plate that we must rely on tricks and shortcuts to get work done. But when the diagnosis becomes the whole of who a person is, it becomes more difficult for that person to have a voice. Even without the help of technology, we categorize, judge, and assume, and bury any contradictions we may come across in lazy gestalts.

The issue is, it is almost impossible for us to undo this sort of "logical framing" once it occurs. When we strip people of their personalities and mark them instead as mere tasks or objects to be handled, we miss key data points. We misdiagnose and alienate. We degrade any trust that might have existed. And then, inevitably, our work with them suffers. We assume we know more about them than they do themselves, ignoring any protest or disagreement.

Over the course of my training as a medical student, I've grown used to answering multiple-choice questions, each with one correct answer. The single best thing to do. *But Henry rejected that "correct" answer because it didn't fit his own personal story.*

Henry was right, of course, *for him.* His response made me look more closely at the world around me. Where else do we need to remember that we are not robots? Where else do we have to know ourselves as clearly as Henry to make bold decisions that maybe no one but ourselves will understand?

Era of Automation and Digitization: Why Your Customers Need You Now More Than Ever

It's not just health care that's becoming automated: most industries are moving toward digitization. Executives today recognize how the automation of our world holds tremendous opportunities for their businesses, often acting as if that were the only option. Companies from banks to athletic brands to airlines gather data on us. When we search for something on the web, the history of that search follows us, surfacing advertisements based on what the algorithms have learned about our past behavior. Facebook and other social networks deliver content based on our recent clicks. Our Netflix viewing habits dictate the movies and television series that are featured when we look for something new to watch.

> **Your customers have lives beyond their digital footprint, and once you learn more about them, you inspire loyalty.**

Each of us, as consumers, is given decisions to make each day about what products to use, services to purchase, and creative content to experience. Whether it's the type of clothing or car that you buy, the medical or life insurance or mortgage you are deciding on, the food you select at your local grocer, the people you hire, or the art, films, theater, or books you choose to pay attention to, we make hundreds of choices all day long. They range from inconsequential to very influential to you and those around you. And sometimes you will make these decisions based on impulse, fulfilling short-term, immediate needs or what data predicts. You also have other decisions to make about brands that come from a far more meaningful and weightier place.

We've already talked about the growing chaos of the digital world, and it's because of that that we see many consumers becoming more and more distant from brands that rely on entirely automated processes.

People like Henry, people like you, and people like me make emotionally significant decisions based on factors beyond pure data. By inspiring meaningful decisions, you can turn your consumers into lifelong fans.

So how do you achieve this ideal in today's world?

Dehumanization: When the Data Gets It Wrong

When we step toward a future of robots and digitized problem solving, we often sacrifice our individuality and that of our customers. This sacrifice becomes all too apparent *when the data gets it wrong*. Examples of this include:

Medicine: the woman who emigrates from India with a chronic cough and a positive test for antibodies against tuberculosis, as is common in endemic countries. Her clinic doctors treat her with powerful antibiotics, but they miss finding the lung cancer that is growing in her chest. Then what?

Customer service: the man in New Jersey who wants a replacement part for his well-loved outdoor grill but keeps getting stuck in automated survey requests and service chat bots instead of real help. He has family arriving next week to celebrate at the spectacular Fourth of July party he's so famous for, so he decides to ditch the grill he's crazy about for a new grill by another brand. "Life is too short!" he calls out to his wife.

Sales: the business traveler who needs to change her mobile phone plan so that it is cost effective for the month that she will be working in another part of the world. No matter what she does, the mobile carrier's site insists on bringing her to the page that upgrades the yearly plan or the page for upgrading her smartphone. In frustration she gives up and then is shocked a few months later when a bill for hundreds of dollars covering international roaming charges appears.

As a consumer, do you sometimes feel like communications automation has made life difficult? Or like you're just another email address unknowingly added to a list of untold millions of others? You can shout as loud as you want into a satisfaction survey, but do you feel you are being heard? So what do you do?

You might decide, like our New Jersey grill aficionado who takes pride in his cherished cookouts, to move on to the next brand.

What do all of these numbers, lists, and facts mean to you? Does it feel as though companies have turned you and your family into an abstraction? Have they separated themselves from the *you* that is your story? This is the process of dehumanization, depriving you of your ability to have thoughts or feelings of your own.

In short, technology cannot re-create the emotional weight of decisions made by a person who's spent their entire life forming their own personal story.

That essential piece will always be missing when the digital dominates the experience. The only way to reverse the trend is by learning how to explore the emotional significance of the decision that clients have to make through understanding their stories.

That's where narrative comes in.

How Narrative Medicine Makes the Big Difference in Health Care

Henry's oncologist, Dr. Raza, was the doctor who freed him to make his own medical decisions based on more than just the biochemical realities of his disease, and she was the doctor with a passion for poetry whose story I shared in the opening of this book. As I mentioned, Dr. Raza introduced me to the idea that I could be both a scientist and an artist. Throughout the time I worked with her, she was in tune with the differences within each patient she saw and offered them more than the newest clinical trial. She gave them an ear to voice their fears and a venue for hope.

And for her medical students, she taught us a surprising new way modern medicine has developed to push back against the growing reliance on technology.

In the early 2000s, a group of clinicians and scholars teaching at Columbia University from a range of disciplines—literature to medicine to ethics—established the beginnings of a program to counter the idea that signs and symptoms alone rule any interaction with a patient. Instead, this program aimed to treat each person as an individual, using the study of literature and the spoken word as a way to teach the skills needed to understand empathy in patient interactions. They did this because they believed that better care can be achieved if we train physicians to skillfully receive patient stories.

They called this approach narrative medicine.

In 2009, Columbia welcomed its first students into their brand-new master's program devoted to helping medical practitioners to learn and to integrate this concept into their work.

When a patient goes in for a conventional medical consult for a thyroid nodule found during a routine check-up visit with their primary care provider, for example, they may meet with a surgical oncologist who will read the results from the ultrasounds and biopsies and suggest a course of action. It can be a sterile interaction, where a patient may feel they have to say yes to a procedure because the doctor tells them that is what is needed.

However, a doctor versed in the principles of narrative medicine would recognize any nuances of subtext and language in how patients talk about themselves. This surgical oncologist trained in the ideas of narrative medicine has learned to ask specific questions designed to draw out the fears or expectations that his or her patient may have been uncomfortable to discuss. With the questions, the patient would share the things that mattered most to them. What if that patient was a singer who feared the loss of her voice from a procedure, or a young father who lost his own father to cancer and is worried that the doctor might make a mistake with this diagnosis? They want to know that they can trust the doctor and have confidence that the doctor's plan meets their needs. The doctor would know to pause if the patient grows quiet and fidgety, and ask if it would be better if the patient went through their options with a patient advocate—a trusted friend or family member. This ultimately amounts to the medical practitioner having a more in-depth and intimate knowledge of not only the patient's signs and symptoms but also their *story*.

This is more than the simple instruction to *listen*, because, as we all have experienced, listening takes time we don't always have. It is about practicing how to coax the truth from others and see beyond the surface. It is the deep understanding of voice, subtext, and observation that frees these physicians to give the quality of care they had always wanted to give.

Raising the Influence of Teens to Take Charge

One example clinicians see of failure of communication that often leads to subpar health care is the dynamic between adults and adolescents. While teens are still required to get their parents' consent for most things regarding their bodies, they are also old enough to have opinions on what they do and do not want. However, their desires are often drowned out by well-meaning parents, grandparents, or caretakers. Many times, their stories aren't heard or are dismissed as irrelevant.

Shira Cahn-Lipman, manager of youth and professional education at Planned Parenthood League of Massachusetts, works in a program designed specifically to work toward this goal of patient-centered care. The Get Real Teen Council is a peer education group for Boston and Central Massachusetts high school students that empowers teens to spread accurate, unbiased, and useful sexuality education. By training the students to facilitate workshops on how to access reproductive health care for their peers and their communities, they are taking charge of the issues that matter most to them regarding their bodies. They even work with medical professionals such as practicing doctors, nurses, and medical students like me on how best to gather information from and advise young patients who may not be trusting of what these adults have to say.

"The number one thing that's so important and consistent within this program is that we are respecting the rights and abilities of young people to make informed decisions about their own lives, particularly their own sexual health," Cahn-Lipman told us. While the GRTC gives them the resources and the avenues to advocate for themselves, the teens are the ones who decide how they want to spread the message. "The facts are always going to be the facts. It's a matter of presenting that information in a way that's understandable and meaningful to them."

In short, these teens want to be *seen* regarding every part of their identity. In the Get Real Teen Council, that means inclusive language, because the teens that make up the program are incredibly diverse, from their gender identity, to their sexual orientation, to their socio-economic status, to their racial and ethnic background. "It is important that people see themselves reflected back in the products that they're consuming, and in the world," Cahn-Lipman says. For example, seeing African American or Asian teens as the main characters in blockbuster films, or advertising for colleges focused on women scientists. Or in the language physicians use when talking to teens about sexual activity, asking, "Are you interested in men, women, or both?" without judgment. That is what allows them to open up—that hint, or invitation, that gives them the room to express themselves. "When people see themselves in those things, it reinforces that they're important."

In my second year in medical school, I was lucky to have the GRTC come to my campus for a training session for medical professionals. The workshop was to make clear to us what was on the minds of young people. What were the questions they were too scared to ask their pediatricians? What subjects did they feel too self-conscious to disclose to their parents or friends? I learned I would get nowhere handing them a packet of resources and wishing them luck. Instead, these teens wanted us to know more about them and how to collaborate with them.

And I learned the most from the stories these teens told us during these workshops.

One teen told us a story about how her friend found out she was pregnant. "She had no idea what to do. She wasn't going to tell anyone," she said. "But then, she remembered I was part of this group and that I knew how to help her." This member of the GRTC was able to be a confidant to her friend and pass along vital contact information and online resources on her options and where to go next. As she described what it was like to give advice and help her friend, I could see how calm and collected she was, armed with the knowledge she gained from the GRTC. Then, as she flashed her braces as she laughed, I remembered that she was only sixteen.

One boy who stood in the front of the class had a brilliant smile as he pointed to raised hands in the crowd, leading us through exercises with ease. He had the gangly stature of a boy growing fast, all limbs and joints, but he held himself like a professional. "I was so scared of public speaking before this," he confessed. "But it's my third year with this group and I've learned so much." He told us about how being part of the Get Real Teen Council gave him the confidence to not only lead these workshops but also organize new clubs at school and become a leader in his local community. Now kids at school look up to him. "I never realized I could do it all."

The main message I heard over and over was, at the core, that all these teens wanted was to be *heard*, *believed*, and *taken seriously* and that they will come back to an adult for advice and help *if they feel safe*. These teens gave me invaluable insight into a population whose voices are often silenced by being told that because they aren't old enough to sign off on their own care at the doctor's office, they aren't old enough to have an opinion. If they weren't old enough to vote, they shouldn't take part in community organization at all. No adult could have taught me the same thing.

"'Empower' is a word I struggle with sometimes because it implies we are giving them power, but they are already wildly powerful," Cahn-Lipman says. "They have voices and they have all the things they want to say, and all we're able to do is give them the stage."

Because storytelling is not unique to any single profession, the idea of a narrative approach to business can be expanded to include a range of industries. Through the practice of *narrative professionalism*, we can always remember to communicate with our clients as people, each of whom includes a collection of stories rather than simply a string of numbers. By being thoughtful and humble, we can open up many different professions to open and trusting conversations, and gain more accurate knowledge of and respect for one another.

Hearing the Voice and Speaking Up for the Voiceless

We often see examples of dehumanization on company websites or advertisements. "Company X, a leading provider of technologies to improve business process, produces a suite of innovative solutions for next-generation, cost-effective, world-class, high-performance, value-added outcomes." It's so hard to parse what they are trying to say. Language like this, written in corporate jargon gobbledygook, has no meaning. This language is passed over and ignored by the person receiving the email, the company brochure, or the corporate blog.

Why? Because it sounds as if a robot wrote it. It has no individual *voice*.

Think about the difference between an owner's manual for a car and a work of poetry. One is sterile, written by the "company" as a whole rather than an individual, but is meant for a purpose, to provide easily understood instructions. Period. The poetry, on the other hand, is extremely individual. You can almost hear the lilt and sway of someone reading it—a unique voice. It makes us feel emotion in a way an owner's manual never can.

Buzzwords, blather, and babble are the new sterile language, and jargon-laden phrases have become so overused that they are meaning-less. It is everywhere: on government forms, company websites, mar-keting materials, and so much more. We use this language because we wish to be perceived as objective—an instruction manual over a work of art—but so often, all a customer wants is just the opposite.

The problem is we don't see corporate language as written by a *person* anymore, but by a machine. It dehumanizes the author and the company and does the opposite of what we intend. We don't trust words without voice because we are sick of dealing with automated service and impersonal products.

As a consumer, do you sometimes feel as if you were simply a string of numbers?

"Cutting-edge, best-of-breed, mission-critical" language is the re-sult of companies not taking the time to understand the people they serve. They don't understand their buyers, the problems buyers face, or how their product helps solve these problems. They also might not un-derstand themselves. Your clients are not the only ones with a story. You too have something unique to say, and your clients want to know that. They don't need a work of poetry, but they do want your voice—the voice of a human. They want to know what makes you tick and better yet what kinds of things you might have in common.

Triathlon World Champion Becomes a Coach Focused on Humanity

"Passion is everything," world champion athlete Siri Lindley says as she describes how she coaches triathletes to success. "When you're taking on some gigantic goal that demands a lot of discipline, you better have a really powerful reason why it matters to you. In those moments when it's so easy to give up, you have to be deeply connected to your passion to keep going."

She says it isn't the numbers on the clock or the shiny metal at the end of a race that makes people champions. It is the intrinsic desire, unique to each and every athlete, that pushes them to achieve ever higher feats.

Lindley told us about her road to becoming a coach upon retiring. "I was desperate to start sharing my message about the importance of experiencing the gift of the journey, because I knew it would change people's lives like it changed mine," she says. "I knew it would help them light a spark inside and believe in themselves." Her incredible passion for her sport resulted in her dominating the International Triathlon Union (ITU) world rankings by winning thirteen World Cup races between 2000 and 2002. After she retired from competition at number one in the world, she also took what she learned about being the best in the world to coach others, inspiring them to look beyond the numbers on their smart watches and instead to understand their own humanity and not take it for granted. "When I realized the gift that comes with the journey, all I wanted to do was to share what I learned and give that gift to others."

Lindley began coaching in Boulder, Colorado, in 2003 and since then has helped her athletes to nine world championship crowns and multiple Olympic medals. One such top athlete is Yvonne van Vlerken. She was already competing at the top of the world when she came to Lindley, but her problem was that she had lost her drive for the sport. She couldn't get excited about getting out of bed to do the hard work and go to the races. She didn't know what was wrong with her. What Lindley said to her as soon as she joined was, "Get rid of the gadgets, we're going to get back to enjoying the sport you love."

Rather than focusing on data and analytics and a worship of numbers, like many other coaches, Lindley teaches athletes to reach inside themselves. Van Vlerken had lost herself in the numbers, becoming discouraged by power meters and heart rate monitors and feeling constantly judged by the data. "I hate that, because when you train and when you race, you should be coming from your heart. From your soul. Expressing your passion. Being brave. Being courageous," Lindley says.

Lindley helped Van Vlerken regain her love of the sport before thinking about competition. Together, they found the spark that she had when she first started competing. Now, after tapping back into the passion for her sport, she has more under-nine-hour Ironman finish times than any athlete, which makes her the most consistently successful Ironman triathlete in the world. She did that by pushing herself *beyond* what she thought she could do by numbers alone, every single day, and it brought back her joy.

Another example is Mirinda Carfrae, four-time world champion, three times at Ironman and one at the 70.3 distance. Carfrae was struggling with using a power meter on her bike that measured wattage of output during practice or a race. It not only discouraged her when the numbers weren't where she wanted them to be, but it was also limiting her. She had stopped being able to feel what her true hardest effort was. "It was killing her, mentally," Lindley says. "A number can become a ceiling if an athlete is too focused on it and it alone."

So Lindley made her stop looking at the power meter. She trained her to get stronger with her knowledge of her own body—understanding what an eight-out-of-ten effort feels like compared with a ten-out-of-ten effort. Then, *the speed came after.*

In 2014, Carfrae won her second world championship Ironman in Kona. During her race, she did have a power meter on her bike, but she didn't look at it. Not even once. Afterward, other athletes and coaches asked to see the numbers she recorded. "They wrote back saying this was the most perfect power file they've ever seen," Lindley says. "They asked how she was using the power meter in her training, but the fact was, we weren't using it at all."

As we write this, of all the hundreds of triathlon clubs that participate in the Ironman Triathlon series, Team Sirius Tri Club is ranked as the number one club in the United States and number three in the world based on points earned by members in races. All this is based not on numbers but on the individual needs and knowledge of her athletes.

You may be asking yourself, What does the success of these individual athletes have to do with my business?

A fandom business is human centered instead of data obsessed.

What Lindley described as important in cultivating the coach-athlete relationship to best serve the athlete was similar to how I viewed the doctor-patient relationship: cultivating the spark by looking at the individual rather than at the numbers and encouraging the athlete to find their own personal reasons to move forward. If each story is different, so are their motivations—their *reasons* for listening. Both doctors and coaches connect with the people who come to them for help by discovering their motivations, and it is that deep understanding that allows both athlete and patient to flourish. Lindley had found that essential element of success by ignoring the buzz of technology to reach deep down inside each individual athlete.

"We all have passion inside of us, but what ignites that passion is different for each of us," she told us. "So businesses need to know how to appeal to every type of customer, and also need to know that we aren't all motivated or inspired about the same things. But that doesn't mean you can't make your business or product attractive to all those people. It's understanding the different desires that are out there and be[ing] able to market for each type of person.".

Halfway through my third year of medical school, I was struggling with my place on the care team. I still felt a little lost. It took another patient to remind me of the power there is in the simple act of listening to a story.

During my time working in adult inpatient medicine, a patient— we'll call him Jeremy—came in overnight, and I was to interview him before the whole medical team saw him. When I went to find him, however, he wasn't in his room. I waited, looking through his chart to get ready. I read in his report that Jeremy had been in and out of homeless shelters for years. He was a paraplegic from a decade-old gunshot wound and was with us for treatment for his recurrent drug-resistant urinary tract infection (UTI).

I visited his room a second time, but he still wasn't there. The nurse came by and told me he'd left, and she wasn't sure where he'd gone. Honestly? I didn't think he'd be back. I read the emergency department notes and thought maybe he had other things waiting for him outside the hospital. At Boston Medical Center, the conditions we treat are as much social as biological, so I knew there might be many other factors complicating his care. I sensed that a UTI probably wasn't high on his priorities.

However, Jeremy *did* return, eventually. I had to hold back my frustration as I greeted him midafternoon. Where had he gone? If he wanted to be treated, why did he think he could come and go as he pleased? I proceeded to ask him a few quick questions—Did he feel feverish? Did the pain track up to his back?—before examining him, yet he stopped me before I got too far.

"Tell me," he said. "What's going on? I took my medications like they said. Why aren't I getting better?"

My stethoscope swung in my hand. No matter how many times I'd reminded myself to listen to the patient, trained myself to avoid stereotyping, I still slipped up sometimes. I realized instantly that by merely checking off a list of symptoms instead of taking the time to pay attention to everything else—how he was speaking to me, what he had done when he was gone, and what he wasn't saying—I was taking the easy way out. Yet no one else would have called me on it, because it's widely accepted behavior, right? I already knew he had pyelonephritis, that was the easy part of this hospital visit. I could hear Henry's voice, saying not to be a robot, reminding me that the most important part of care is *this*, finding out his story.

I responded to Jeremy's why as best I could. I spoke about bacteria and drugs and what was to come, as though it were a new subject, then waited as he digested the information. He nodded slowly and looked me in the eye. In an instant, I saw something there that I didn't expect to see—*patience*. Patience mixed with a true desire to understand me.

"Nobody had ever told me that," he said. He frowned. "Can I ask another question?"

I could feel my own demeanor shift in that moment. I had time. I didn't have a teaching session for another few hours, and the residents supervising me knew I was with this patient. "Yes, Jeremy," I replied. "Ask me about whatever you want to know."

Your relationship with your customer starts with your curiosity about them.

He told me about himself and his frustrations, what was important to him and what was not. Then he told me his whole story.

Jeremy did end up staying for the duration of his treatment. It wasn't because of the fancy diagnostic equipment or the high-powered drugs. It was because he reorganized his priorities. He *chose* to stay.

During the week he was with us, we switched his meds three times as his cultures came back with more aggressive bacteria than we first thought. He stayed through our apologies that the antibiotics would have to be given intravenously and that he would have to stay just a little longer to make sure that was done properly.

He stayed, and when he was done, he asked that I be the one to take out his midline catheter from his vein. Not the attending physician, who had the final say in his medications, nor the interns who signed the orders. Simply because I had taken the time to talk to him and find out what mattered to *him*, he asked for *me*.

When Jeremy scooted out of the hospital on his motorized wheelchair, he stopped to say goodbye to me. "Thank you for everything you did for me," he said. "I *really* appreciate it."

All I had done was learn his story, not from the chart or from the textbook, but from him to me, face-to-face.

I listened and I learned.

And to Jeremy, that was what made all the difference.

CHAPTER 11

Tell the Truth, Especially When It Hurts

by David

During a typical day, our letter carrier drops off around a dozen pieces of mail that we bring in from our mailbox to be sorted on the dining table. Direct mailers for products and services we're not interested in, like a catalog for bedsheets, or a flyer from a real estate agent who wants to list our house for sale, end up in the recycling bin.

Other solicitations include stock photographs of people who look nothing like me, Yukari, our neighbors, or anybody we know. The dentist's mailer with a "customer" portrait depicting the perfect Hollywood-ready family fresh from a trip to a beauty salon. Even their groomed, pedigreed chocolate Labrador retriever has flawless white teeth. Or the financial services company trying to get my retirement planning business by sending me a postcard with a trim older couple wearing all white while on a carefree stroll along a pristine powdery white sand beach, framed by swaying palm trees in the distance. I'm thinking to myself, "There's no way those people are really your customers!" Those get recycled too.

We also receive solicitations in the mail that stretch the truth to ensnare the gullible or contain outright lies. Here are a few things that arrived in the past week: A window-style envelope containing what looks exactly like a check. When opened, it is a credit card offer. An official-looking manila envelope stamped "Critical Documents—Open Immediately" but that contains yet another solicitation for a credit card. Even companies I already do business with get into the stretching-the-truth game and act like I haven't been their customer for the past twenty years. My bank sends my monthly statement marked "Important: Do Not Destroy." I destroy it because I've already seen my statement online.

And then there's the trickery that arrives via phone calls. The "free one-week cruise to the Caribbean" that I've won. The person who says I owe the IRS money and they're ready to help.

We get so many of these sorts of phone calls and emails and direct mail solicitations that we've almost become used to lies. No wonder you overhear people say: "Is what these companies say actually true?"

We've been lied to so many times by the companies we do business with that we are attuned to falsehoods. Our instinctive reactions tell us to stay away.

IHOP: #IHOb and Lying to Your Fans

These direct mailers and phone calls are techniques that too many organizations use to communicate with their customers. They deploy language that we assume isn't true. It doesn't feel authentic.

Here are statements that we frequently see or hear that, like the typical direct mail piece, we simply don't believe anymore. (We construct our own personal truths in our heads to what we assume are untruths.)

- "Your call is important to us." (Yeah, right. Then why doesn't someone answer the phone?)
- "Due to higher than expected call volume, your wait time is longer than normal." (Why is it *always* higher than expected? Shouldn't you hire more reps?)
- "We love our customers." (Can you *just feel the love*?)
- "Supplies are running low!" (Of this old product we're trying to get rid of.)
- "This is the best price I can offer." (Unless you turn us down, of course.)
- "My husband was the Oil Minister of an African country and he recently died. I need the help of someone trustworthy to transfer $15 million from his account and in return I will give you a large fee." (Yep. So why are you in Eastern Europe?)

It also seems that not very many people believe what our leaders say. Politics has become theater. When politicians run for office, they make promises that they assume voters *know* they won't keep. Then, when they are elected, many will say just about anything they want because they don't fear repercussions. And when they are being interviewed, their handlers tell them their most important job is to keep the viewer from picking up the remote control to change the channel.

Lying in public is now so widespread that some marketers even feel free to use it as a ploy to get attention. "Fake news" is so widespread it's a joke.

For example, social media exploded with the news, released June 4, 2018, that IHOP (International House of Pancakes) was to change its name a few days later to "IHOb." The company made an announcement via a new verified Twitter feed at @IHOb:

For 60 pancakin' years, we've been IHOP. Now, we're flippin'
our name to IHOb. Find out what it could b on 6.11.18. #IHOb

"IHOb" retweeted an image of a crane replacing an IHOP sign with
an IHOb one, making more plausible the idea that it was changing its
name.

Many IHOP fans shared their deep concern on social media. They
wanted to know: What's going on with the brand we love? Thousands
of fans didn't like the impending name change one bit, and they said
things on social media like:

- "IHOP is changing its name to IHOB and while people think it
  stands for "breakfast" I'm putting my money on BETRAYAL"
- "just found out ihop is changing their name to ihob and I
  feel like many of my constitutional rights are being violated"
- "IHOP JUST CHANGED IT'S NAME TO IHOB?! THEY
  ARE FAMOUS FOR PANCAKES, MAN. PANCAKES!"

Others said things on social media specifically calling out the marketers involved:

- "International House of Bad marketing decisions"
- "I want to be a fly on the wall at the marketing meetings"
- "Dear @IHOb Changing from a proven business model and
  going in a new direction is a great idea. Regards, New Coke"

Many mainstream media outlets were sucked in and published sto-
ries about the impending name change including *The Washington
Post*, Florida's *Sun Sentinel* newspaper, Yahoo!, CNN, and several local
ABC and CBS network-affiliated television stations.

Some people tried to guess what "IHOb" could mean. Many guessed "International House of Bacon." Others got cute, suggesting weird things like "International House of Björk" and "International House of Bitcoin." Chiquita tweeted "International House of Bananas" and the musician Brian Eno tweeted "International House of Brian Eno."

Some of the burger chains jumped in with some clever newsjacking. Burger King even temporarily changed its name on social media to "Pancake King."

@Wendys got a nice dig in by tweeting:

> Remember when you were like 7 and thought changing your name to Thunder BearSword would be super cool? Like that, but our cheeseburgers are still better.

@Whataburger:

> As much as we love our pancakes, we'd never change our name to Whatapancake.

Then, on June 11, 2018, IHOb, er . . . IHOP let the world know the answer.

Just kidding!

IHOP admitted it wasn't really going to change its name. It turns out it was simply a stunt to get social media talking about the fact that you can go to IHOP for more than just breakfast and, oh yeah, they now have burgers too.

It turns out that for IHOP, lying was a marketing strategy. However, this approach to business repelled fans—its best customers.

Sure, the IHOb thing was just a marketing gimmick. You might say, "Lighten up, David."

Yes, it got attention.

However, the idea of messing with the truth when communicating with the loyal fans of your company and its products is deception—not good marketing. And not the way to build a fanocracy. This story underlines the significance of trust and whether people will associate a brand with the things that trust engenders.

When I shared my thoughts on the situation on social media, these were among the comments I received:

- "iHOP traded trust for some publicity. The publicity will disappear in a day or so, but the trust will disappear faster, and is much harder to regain."
- "Feels like they cried 'Wolf'. Not going to listen again."
- "Why not April 1st? Maybe they thought they were too clever with this one to even wait for April Fool's Day."
- "So, is Paul really dead?"

Over the course of many interactions taking months or years, a customer learns what a brand stands for. In the case of a restaurant, the brand also becomes such things as cleanliness, the demeanor of the staff, the quality of the food, and much more. Over dozens of visits that could span decades, generations of people come know the kind of experience to expect. The relationship between a brand and its customers is a complicated one. Building trust takes time.

This is true of every entity, whether it's a restaurant, hotel, airline, software product, vehicle, actor, singer, salesperson, consultant, banker, stockbroker, critic, doctor, or a TV, film, or Broadway show, and so on. We all have to focus on building a reputation with those who do business with us.

> ## Building trust is an essential ingredient in creating a fanocracy.

With our easy access to the web as a way to research alternatives, the market for all products and services and experiences is crowded with competitors. If you lose well-earned trust from the consumers you serve, then it's never been easier for people to switch. Also, it doesn't take much time for them to complain. Seconds. All it takes is a tweet.

There are many problems with gaming social media in the way that IHOP/IHOb did. Once you've made lying your business strategy, if you have a crisis, your social channels are a lot less likely to help you manage the situation. In the case of IHOP, if people were to become sickened in a restaurant, would it be difficult for them to use social media in a convincing way during the next crisis?

Will anyone believe them *this time*?

People at organizations cannot play fast and loose with the truth and keep their fans, their clients, and customers loyal. Contrast the way that IHOP communicated with fans with how another popular restaurant chain chose to do so. The difference was startlingly simple. The difference was truth.

KFC: The Chicken Restaurant That Ran Out of Chicken

It was a #KFCCrisis! A chicken restaurant without any chicken!

One otherwise fine day in 2018, KFC ran out of chicken in the UK. KFC had changed logistics companies, and the new provider fouled up the fowl deliveries.

KFC could have ducked the chicken problem or hid behind gobble-dygook words or blamed the logistics company, the sorts of actions we expect. Instead of the typical response, KFC did a wonderful job communicating on social networks and via advertisements, using humor to get people interested but providing valuable information to its fans, those who frequent the company's restaurants.

In UK newspapers, the company ran full-page advertisements cleverly changing the KFC logo on a chicken bucket to FCK. One of the ads read:

> We're sorry. A chicken restaurant without any chicken. Huge apologies to our customers, especially those who travelled out of their way to find we were closed. And endless thanks to our KFC team members and our franchise partners for working tirelessly to improve the situation. It's been a hell of a week, but we're making progress, and every day more and more fresh chicken is being delivered to our restaurants. Thank you for bearing with us.

The company quickly created a website to provide a list of all UK restaurants and the chicken status of each. It also offered rewards to people affected via the company smartphone app.

On social media, the company was constantly providing updates, many with the fun approach of the ads.

Based on the reactions on social media, KFC did an excellent job handling this crisis. The company was quick to communicate, it was transparent in telling customers what was happening, and it did so in an engaging way. And when chicken started being served again, all was forgiven.

When you engage with your fans, always tell the truth.

There is no other choice than to tell the truth when your fans deserve to know what's happening. You don't gloss over the negative, you face it right off, you are clear and specific. There are many different approaches to this, including the humor we especially enjoy that was used by KFC.

Blockchain Technology as a Critical Ingredient of Trust

Maintaining transparency and always telling the truth will be a key ingredient in building your fanocracy. When your fans know they can always rely on you to be open and honest, even when you make a mistake (especially when you make a mistake), they will honor and respect you and be eager to do business with you.

There are many organizations quietly telling the truth and building transparency into the way they do business. Their customers notice and come back for more. Many remain loyal fans, and over time, fanocracies develop.

Considered the original superfood, olive oil has a rich and colorful history. Edible olives were grown in ancient Crete in 3500 BC, and Romans started cultivating olive groves to harvest the oil in about 600 BC. However, the modern olive oil business is fraught with misleading advertising, confusing claims, bad information, and outright lies about the origin and freshness of the oil. Sometimes it's not even oil from olives. Some producers cheat their customers by cutting olive oil with other oils like soybean or sunflower, some dilute high-quality olive oil with low-quality olive oil, and some misrepresent the country of origin by, say, labeling low-grade oil from another country as being from Italy.

The sobering nature of this reality holds great significance for Julie Harnish, founder and CEO of Veritat Olive Oil. *Veritat* means "truth" in Catalan, and her oil is imported directly from the Priorat region of Spain. While living in Barcelona with her family years ago, Harnish was always careful about the foods that she fed to her four young children. She became a big fan of a local brand of olive oil and loved the taste so much that she researched the origin of the oil, met the producers, and learned about production. When her kids grew older, she realized that olive oil had become her passion, so she began conducting olive oil tastings for friends in Barcelona.

Encouraged by what she learned about people's likes and dislikes, she was soon bottling and selling olive oil and, as she did so, developed deep personal relationships with her early customers, hand-selling to her friends to launch the company. When she moved to the United States, she established a company to import Spanish olive oil and develop a brand to sell it at retail and mail order.

"It's important that olive oil be fresh because olive oil goes rancid," Harnish told us. "It deteriorates after eighteen months to two years depending on how it is stored. Rancid oil won't kill you and it doesn't make you sick, it just tastes bad and that's part of the problem, because there isn't a big incentive [by unscrupulous olive oil producers] to have fresh oil. I really care about what is going into each and every person's body. I don't know if I get it from being a mom. But I feel responsible for what I say is in the bottle is actually in there and you can trust it and you know where it's coming from."

It's also important for Harnish to develop trust because Veritat sells single-cultivar olive oil. Like wines made with different varieties of grapes, most commercial olive oils are blends. And just as different varieties of grapes produce certain flavors in wine, olive cultivars create specific characteristics in olive oils. "I find that singles are much more exciting and have many more layers of taste," she says. As such, her customers rely on her label to be accurate. That leads to much repeat business and a strong camaraderie and mutual support among single-cultivar producers and the chefs and bottlers who buy from them.

However, high-quality oils don't come cheap. "It's hard to compete with olive oils that cost ten dollars when the real cost for getting single cultivar into the US is triple that," she says.

Harnish now takes her devotion to truth to the extreme, relying on blockchain (a cryptography technology) to track oil from the olive tree to the consumer's dinner table. Each bottle includes a QR code that the customer can scan. They are then taken to a page where all the details of their particular bottle are available, including the date and time the olives were picked, the location of the tree, the baskets they were in, when they were at the mill being processed into paste, when the oil was separated out, when it was bottled, when it reached the port in Barcelona, and when it reached the port in the United States. Through the retail shipper tracking systems, Harnish also has the ability to know the exact date and time a package of olive oil arrived at a consumer's home.

It's the first time this tree-to-table process has been tracked via blockchain in the olive oil industry. Despite demanding a higher price than most olive oil brands, Harnish's business is flourishing.

And what winds up being the key ingredient to this success? What is it that she does to convey the honesty that can live up to the company name?

Transparency.

This is what the blockchain technology and everything else she creates around her business model ultimately ensures: that consumers know all they can about the products they're purchasing from her. Harnish found that being open and honest with her customers has been good for business. She's used this openness as a business differentiator in her marketplace, and because it is so rife with cheating, it provides a great way to grow fans.

Harnish's work with Veritat demonstrates the incredible power of telling the truth. Her example places a focus on what a business can do for their fan base first, rather than just doing what brings the best short-term results, like many other companies selling inferior or mislabeled oil.

Of course, not every product or service lends itself to the extreme transparency of Harnish's technology-based solution for sharing the journey of her olive oil from the olive tree to a customer's door. However, a focus on transparency can benefit any organization. As we've said before, when you earn the trust of your fans, people will stay with you during difficult times.

Concert Ticketing: Establishing and Sustaining Trust with Your Fans

As people evaluate an organization they are considering doing business with (or, similarly, deciding which school to attend, nonprofit to donate to, entertainment to experience, or politician to vote for), they have to feel they can trust that organization. Today as people evaluate making a purchase from, investing in, getting involved with, or working for an organization, they usually consider the entity's website, social media, online reviews, a physical store, office, or warehouse, and what the people they encounter who represent the company are like.

> **Be consistent in your behavior and you can win the trust of your customers.**

How can old and new entities or brands establish trust in something they're about to introduce to the marketplace? It's as simple as putting fans first, and being truthful and honest about your business practices.

Are you a live music fan like Reiko and me? Like us, do you get frustrated at the difficulty of purchasing good seats to the shows and concerts you are eager to see? We've found the ticketing process for many shows is murky at best, yet some popular acts work hard to ensure that the best seats get into the hands of the biggest fans.

In some cases, this means less revenue for the artist in the short term. However, by helping the average fan to get a ticket at a reasonable price, that band's fans will continue to come back year after year, tour after tour, meaning that fan ultimately puts more money in the artist's bank account than if the fan had been gouged early on.

It's worth taking a look at how ticketing works in America and considering how some bands have approached the process to create a fanocracy. The methods used here can help us find ways to build transparency and truth into our own businesses.

Most bands put their tickets for shows up for sale on Ticketmaster or other electronic sales outlets knowing that the best seats will be snapped up by ticket brokers using bots that automatically purchase tickets and then resell them at a markup on third-party sites like StubHub. It has become standard industry practice. Yet as a fan, do you get frustrated when you log in to a ticket service the first second a hot show goes on sale and find the system only has seats available in the second balcony of the theater or the top tier of the arena? When that happens, do you want to buy? What's even more frustrating is when you go to StubHub or other ticket broker sites and see that hundreds or even thousands of the best seats to the show, which you weren't able to get, are available at prices double or triple face value, sometimes more. How does that make you feel?

Sadly, many bands are complicit in this practice and hold back their own tickets for resale on secondary markets. They profit while their biggest fans are left irritated and confused. Band management often has a short-term, take-the-easy-way-out mentality. It's a lot easier and less risky for them to let the brokers take thousands of seats, because those brokers then take the risk if the show does not prove popular. It's not uncommon for brokers to dump tickets at a loss when the show date comes near for shows that don't sell well. Needless to say, this practice by bands and their managers does not build a loyal fan base.

Some bands blame the brokers, the bots, and the electronic ticket services, saying their hands are tied and they can't combat the practice of the best tickets going to scalpers. Yet they do have a choice. If they took it as their responsibility to treat their fans right, they could build a fanocracy that would last for years, or even decades.

However, there are positive things happening on the ticketing front with many bands, their management, and the ticketing industry working to solve the problem.

In 2016, Ticketmaster launched Verified Fan, a service that uses an algorithm to determine who among its customers are actual fans versus bots (or people) who buy tickets for resale. I have purchased tickets to many shows using Verified Fan, and it works well. When the super-popular Broadway show *Hamilton* came to Boston, I was able to get the hot tickets through Ticketmaster Verified Fan. The platform knows, through my buying behavior over the years, that I am a music fan, and therefore I got a special code.

However, only a few hundred artists are using the system as we write this. It's up to the artists to sign up to be a part of Verified Fan to treat fans with respect. Bruce Springsteen, for example, used Verified Fan for tickets to his run of hugely popular Broadway shows. According to *Rolling Stone*, only 3 percent of those tickets were resold on the secondary markets, indicating that Springsteen's fans were in the house with tickets they purchased directly. Other acts experimenting with Verified Fan to bypass the multibillion-dollar ticket-scalping business include Pearl Jam, Tom Waits, Jack White, Ed Sheeran, and Harry Styles.

Some artists are experimenting with other ways to combat the ticketing problem and are transparent about how they sell tickets.

Enlightened artists have gone to paperless ticketing, which requires fans to show identification (typically an ID or the credit card used to purchase the tickets) at the entrance for admittance. This approach means that the fan who purchased the original ticket (plus those who are entering together with the ticket purchaser) is the only one who can use it to get in. However, this approach can mean long lines to get into a venue because each person needs to be checked at the door.

Other artists have set up fan clubs that offer members first crack at tickets for shows. The National's Cherry Tree, Dave Matthews Band's Warehouse, and Jack White's Vault are examples of clubs where fans pay a yearly membership fee and are given preferred access to tickets to shows.

Another approach is to use dynamic pricing, similar to how airlines price seats. Prices change as the show gets closer, and fans can choose when to pay. Like on an airplane, the person sitting next to you might have paid a different price, but by ticketing in this way, fans buy tickets on the primary market with the revenue going to the artists. The Rolling Stones have been using dynamic pricing for recent tours, and they are open and transparent about how they price. When shows are announced, fan club members are the first to have access, followed by the public. But even to their fans, the best tickets are very expensive during the start of sales, much like the business class seats available on international flights six months from a travel date. If you want to lock in the best seats, great, but you have to pay up. The Stones try to price near what the secondary market would bear for the seats closer to the stage, with some of the best going for over a thousand dollars each. Then, just like frequent airline fare sales, unsold Stones tickets are offered to fans a few weeks before the show. During the last tour, the band offered a "Lucky Dip" ticket system where people could purchase a pair of tickets at a reasonable price, but they did not know where they would sit until they arrived at the venue. The two people had to show up together, the purchaser presented ID, and the random pair of tickets were provided on the spot. The twist was that the ticket holders had to enter the venue immediately, ensuring that the tickets weren't resold outside.

The ticketing industry has a way to go to earn back the respect of fans.

Soon they'll realize that when the best fans get the best seats, everybody wins. Creating a fanocracy by authentically working with fans, understanding their frustrations, and demonstrating how important they are is good business.

Stop Spinning, Start Connecting, and Begin to Change the World

Have you reached a point where you expect the worst in the companies you do business with? Do you throw corporate statements that come in the mail out with the trash? Do you anticipate being taken advantage of? Do you ever assume that companies you do business with won't respond quickly and that when they do, they either won't be honest or will somehow manipulate the truth?

In a world of increasing scandal, with institutions playing fast and loose with the truth and people slapping "fake news" labels on content with increasing frequency, there is an alarmingly simple approach that companies and other entities can embrace so as to sustain the trust they've built over what may be decades.

And that is to simply own up to mistakes, struggles, obstacles, errors, or other problematic situations in real time. Your fans deserve it.

Rather than delaying responses, finding flimsy spin words, and obscuring compromising procedures from the view of customers, instead allow success to come from an embrace of transparency. Social media and other outlets are ideal to continually engage with followers with a reaffirming presence—especially when things go wrong.

When you encounter a person or an organization treating you honestly and fairly, aren't you excited? When you are told the truth, even if you don't like it at first, do you feel respected? And when you encounter this kind of company, are you happy to do business with it again and again? And are you more apt to tell your friends about it too?

As I was sorting my mail recently, I came across yet another catalog. However, this particular one didn't end up in the recycling bin. This was from an organization that I knew told the truth, and therefore I was excited to flip through it.

Deutsche Optik sells surplus gear, often from militaries from around the world. The Deutsche Optik catalog is written by founder Justus Bauschinger, and he publishes his photo and email address on the first page in case you want to reach out to him. I just love his approach to telling the truth. His opening letter in the winter 2018 catalog included this:

I've found a bunch more great stuff to spread throughout these pages for you. Bunch of Swiss, Czech, Yugoslav, and even U.S. stuff. We are also running low on vintage microscopes and typewriters, and when they're gone, that'll be it. We have exhausted our sources. But there will always be more desirable stuff to be found, and I'll be on my way to Europe in late January to do some serious pillaging for you.

I know from experience that Deutsche Optik is honest. When Bauschinger says supplies are running low, it isn't a lie to get me to buy. It's the truth.

The catalog descriptions Bauschinger writes frequently make me laugh out loud. They are so honest it might even be embarrassing for some people to read. For example, this description of the company's Italian Navy Pea Coats (I've edited out a few sentences for length):

> Wow. . ! As you know we rarely do items of dress in our catalogs, because of the sizing issues, but every now and again, something so spectacular comes our way, that we cannot resist . . . As with the French Alpine Troops wool capes, a couple of years ago, these Italian Navy Pea Coats make us priapic . . . It is as though someone like Giorgio Armani or Ermenegildo Zegna design the uniforms for the Italian Military! . . . Boy. . , our Navy's pea coats don't hold a candle to these gorgeous coats. . . .
>
> *Please note: these Pea Coats are for the slender, if you have a beer-gut hanging, they won't fit!*

Amazing. The founder of Deutsche Optik not only uses the word "priapic" in a description of a coat in his catalog, he also warns that if you have a beer gut, it won't fit you. Who does that? Maybe we all should! It's so refreshing and appealing.

I've been a Deutsche Optik fan for decades.

Bauschinger communicates with perfect (some might say brutal) honesty and beautiful transparency. And that's why he's so irresistible!

CHAPTER 12

Develop Employees Who Are Fans

by David

When I was in Rome in early 2018 to deliver a presentation, I had a free day to explore the city. When lunchtime came, I checked out about a dozen places to eat the old-school, analog way—wandering around, looking in windows, and perusing menus. I chose Cajo & Gajo at Piazza di San Calisto in the funky Trastevere neighborhood because it looked warm and welcoming and was very reasonably priced.

Since the restaurant was in an area frequented by tourists, and because the signs were in English, I was prepared for a decent meal, but nothing special, having dined at many such places that don't rely on repeat business. Therefore, my expectation was that the service would likely be mediocre. Who cares, right? It wasn't, after all, going to be the last meal I'd ever have.

What first caught my eye was the hand-drawn sign in multicolor chalk on a large vintage wood-framed blackboard just outside the restaurant. It was filled with whimsical drawings—musical notes, a full carafe, and a smiley face beside HAPPY HOUR (LITRE OF WINE = TEN EURO) AND FREE WiFi. Amused, I couldn't help but smile as I stepped toward the restaurant entrance.

Soon I was greeted with "Hi there! I'm Gaetano. Would you prefer to sit outside or inside?"

"It's a beautiful day here, but cold back in Boston where I live," I said. "Outside please."

"It's always beautiful in Roma!" Gaetano laughed as he swept his hand to indicate the several open tables on the cobblestone sidewalk. Potted plants, umbrellas, and wooden boxes filled with empty wine bottles served as decoration. Fit and thirtyish with a week's growth of scruff on his face, Gaetano wore black pants, a black turtleneck shirt with a Cajo & Gajo logo, and a bright red apron sporting the name of a wine producer. "Your choice. Most people prefer outside with a view of the piazza," he said, and then pointed toward the door to the restaurant. "But, if you change your mind, we've got tables inside too. Ah! Here's Maria. We'll be taking care of you this afternoon!"

The experience at Cajo & Gajo exceeded my expectations. The fun-loving staff—Gaetano, Maria, and their colleagues—made the experience exciting and memorable. They clearly love their work. They smiled the whole time! When they had a free moment, they quietly sang along to the music and danced a little too. They laughed and joked with the group of three couples next to me, and their enthusiasm got the group to order another bottle of wine. The patter never felt forced or memorized, it was as if they were having fun with friends over a meal in their home.

When I finished my lunch, I was surprised with a glass of free limoncello and cookies for dessert. Wow! What a nice extra!

I asked if I could take their photo, and they good-naturedly struck a pose: three people close to one another on the steps leading to the inside of the restaurant all making a heart sign with their fingers and all smiling and laughing. I had such a wonderful experience that I realized they were the living, breathing epitome of fanocracy!

The food was good, but let's face it, lots of restaurants in Rome have good food. The piazza where my table was located was picturesque, however I've seen many that are more interesting and beautiful.

It was the experience I had with a group of truly passionate people that converted me into a fan of the Cajo & Gajo restaurant.

After I returned to my hotel that evening, I popped over to Trip-Advisor to see what other diners thought. I wasn't surprised to see that Cajo & Gajo was rated number 52 of 10,578 restaurants in Rome. That put it in the top 1 percent! It's interesting that nearly every one of the first few pages of the more than 10,000 reviews included words like "friendly" and "kind" to describe the service and staff, usually before people even described anything about the food.

Cajo & Gajo built its fanocracy primarily from how its staff interacts with customers. Enthusiastic staff is just one element of a restaurant, and it's a powerful way to stand out and build a loyal fan base. It didn't have a celebrity chef and wasn't in the most crowded or most exclusive neighborhood, yet its staff delivered an enjoyable personal experience to customers like me. What a great way to build a business! When you are treated well by enthusiastic employees, isn't it a joy?

As the data from TripAdvisor shows, having passionate people represent your brand is great for your business.

Are Your Employees Feeling Their Significance?

It has become tremendously popular for companies to invest significant sums of money into developing an "organizational culture." They want a culture that inspires employees to become such devoted fans that they share their fandom with the outside world. However, that investment can often come across as phony. Incentivized motivation for employee participation, or gimmicks like requiring people to wear company-branded polo shirts or participate in employee team barbecues in the summer can sometimes lack the kind of authentic joy and enthusiasm I enjoyed in Rome at Cajo & Gajo.

In the long run, artificial approaches don't work and can become counterproductive. Employees who might have had a strong passion about where they work will resent a forced, fake-cheerful approach. They crave the real. We all do.

Again, I became an instant fan of Cajo & Gajo *not* because of the food or the view but rather because of the way its staff engaged with me. They built a personal connection with me while I was at their restaurant enjoying my meal. That experience of a passionate restaurant staff being themselves—singing and dancing, personally drawing the menu, making the heart sign with their fingers in photos, and telling silly jokes, all while making customers feel like family—was extraordinary. The staff of Cajo & Gajo probably never, ever saw themselves as "fanocracy builders," yet they were, and by the looks of other patrons, they made a huge difference to everyone lucky enough to be there with me!

Authentic advocacy from inside your organization will inspire the enthusiasm, enjoyment, and passion that create a fanocracy.

Customers already expect to find people who are "just doing their job." Yet when an employee shows strong passion about what they are doing, it's infectious. Everything is affected—the work and the people involved are immediately engaged. It's essential in building your fanocracy.

Creating a Winning Team!

"When you're late in the race, your body is absolutely screaming at you and just saying 'Dude, why?'" says Pete Cipollone, coxswain of the world-record-setting 2004 Athens Olympic gold medal US men's eight rowing team. He competed in the 2000 Sydney Olympics, was a coach in the 1996 Atlanta Olympics, and is a four-time world rowing champion. "But you're starting to pick up momentum. Every stroke you take is you getting closer to the finish line. And you're moving through your competition, or you're moving away, and there is a really strange sensation, on one side you have the pain that is just telling you to stop and on the other side you're saying 'No, I want to go more. I want to try to destroy myself. I want to find what my outer limit is.' That is the ecstatic moment of rowing because every aspect of yourself is turned up to eleven at that point. Your body is screaming at you to stop and your mind is saying 'No, go for more,' and then the subconscious is wondering 'How far can I push this?'"

One of Cipollone's most memorable races was the 1997 Head of the Charles, where he was coxswain of the US Rowing entry in the men's eight. A rowing journalist had asked if he could place a tape recorder in the boat to record Cipollone's race call, and Cipollone agreed.

Guys, listen up, I think you can break the record!
Get ready, get ready . . .
Go now!
Legs!
Legs!
Legs!
That's it!

Legs, send!
Legs, send!
Legs, send!
Driving for that line. Now go!
Push, chaaa!
Push, chaaa!
Push, chaaa!
Going, that's it.

"We won by a ton, we set the course record, and we were the first crew to break fourteen minutes," Cipollone says. "The audio of my call became like a Grateful Dead bootleg. All the coxswains wanted to get a copy of it. And then it went up on the internet and became viral. People come to me, rowers and coxswains alike, and many say 'When I'm working out, I listen to the audio of that race and it gets me so pumped up.' Or they say 'I've been studying everything you ever said, everything you ever wrote about coxing. I'm just a huge fan.'" (You can hear an audio of Cipollone 1997 Head of the Charles race call by searching "Pete Cipollone 1997 HOCR" on YouTube. I've listened a dozen times myself; however, be aware that he uses salty language.)

Passion Is a Habit

Hiring employees to be a part of your team is a pivotal aspect of building any organization. Sadly, most managers and representatives of human resources departments don't bring enough creativity and obvious interest to their own jobs. They can end up following the traditional approach to bringing new people into an organization—they do it "by the book." They obsess over a candidate's education, the companies they once worked for and for how long, and their previous salary. They pore over the résumés, and note or measure the skills. In the interview with the person, questions such as "What are your greatest strengths and weaknesses?" and "Where do you see yourself in five years?" elicit no-win, dead-end responses that no one wants to listen to. Ho-hum. Dullsville. Boring. *Next!*

Cipollone's approach to hiring people to work at his company is very different. He's the founder and CEO of InstaViser, a technology company creating online platforms to support community. His enthusiasm for the sport of rowing makes him a better leader of a technology company. Those two things might seem unrelated, but they're not.

Cipollone hires elite athletes, including other Olympians like himself, to work at InstaViser. Some are retired from competing, yet several are in the middle of intense training for their sport and work at InstaViser part time. He believes something very simple but powerful:

Passion is a habit.

Cipollone places tremendous emphasis on a critical ingredient when he hires: his ideal employees start off with passion before they're hired. They walk in the door dripping with passion and enthusiasm.

Passionate employees are excited about you and their work, and they are eager to tell others.

Cipollone's hiring practices teach us how important it is to cultivate employees who have passion. It doesn't matter what that passion is, as long as the prospective employee lives their *own* life with gusto and is *an enthusiastic fan of something*!

Passion in one part of life predicts passion in other aspects, right? Which makes passionate people ideal employees, because a person like that would never accept a job they weren't excited about.

Meghan O'Leary, Cipollone's vice president in charge of marketing and customer success, is an Olympic rower. Elana Meyers Taylor, Insta-Viser's customer success manager, became famous for appearing in advertisements for Comcast during the 2018 Winter Olympics. She is the number one US bobsled driver, has won four world championships, and is an Olympian with a bronze medal in the 2010 Vancouver games and silver medals in both the 2014 Sochi and the 2018 Pyeongchang games. Kyle Tress, the company's lead developer, was a US Olympic skeleton athlete.

"We are definitely building a very specific corporate culture that's in line with our athletic experiences," Cipollone says. "We hire people who are stoked to be here every day! The athletes we hire have three common traits. They are super goal-oriented, consummate professionals, and outstanding teammates. We understand what the finish lines are. We understand what the milestones are that help us move toward our goal. We want to be extraordinarily good at 'playing our positions,' but perhaps the most important thing is that when we are in the office, we make the people around us better. And this pays off. If you ask any of our customers, they would say that of all the companies that they work with, we are among the most excellent because we understand what they are trying to accomplish."

For Cipollone, hiring other elite athletes has proven to be a winning strategy. "There's no doubt in my mind that investing early—like, at the beginning—in high quality customer success is the reason we have one hundred percent renewals and strong account expansion at renewal time," he says. "Customers pay for expertise, results, and 'no surprises.'"

Other CEOs search for passion of various kinds when they have an open position to fill.

Maybe they wouldn't use the word "passion," yet they want to sense a kind of fire-in-the-belly interest in the person interviewing for a job.

It's amazing to me when I hear about how many people go for an interview without any curiosity or knowledge of the company they've applied to. Today every company has a website that tells its whole story, and lists names of the principals and what they are in charge of. Walking in the door and knowing about a company and its marketplace and history tells a person if he or she is a match. Knowing that makes the interview much easier because the candidate can talk right up front about his or her work history and personal values and say what he or she might bring to the job. The more the candidate knows and helps manage the positive flow of the interview, the better his or her chances are of being seriously considered. In that first interview, candidates have an opportunity to demonstrate how they can add to the fanocracy of any organization.

Corporate and entrepreneurial leaders look for people who are thoughtful and potentially articulate representatives of their company. One such leader is Ryan Caldbeck, cofounder and CEO of CircleUp, a financial technology company based in San Francisco. CircleUp helps early stage consumer brands find and work with investors.

The entire venture capital world is about relationships. Will the investor and the company executive team bond? How do employees facilitate those connections? So the idea of fandom is an interesting way to cement bonds between people.

"Passion is what I look for the most in new teammates or investors," Caldbeck says. "I believe, based on no scientific research at all, that passion is the most important ingredient for success." Caldbeck has a specific formula of three things he uses when interviewing people:

1. Does the person have passion?
2. Do they know what they are passionate about?
3. Is that passion aligned with something that will help further a specific cause?

He says all are great, and if you have all three, you're on track to win. "I'm not alone," he says. "Not every CEO would describe it like this, but their faces light up when they realize you are passionate, you know what you're passionate about, and that passion aligns with the company."

In his work in venture capital, Caldbeck knows the details of what works at many different companies. "I've seen people with zero qualifications get hired at the best companies, break into new industries, and thrive because they demonstrated their passion clearly and it was aligned with what that company needs," he says.

Hiring the right people has been effective for CircleUp. The company has raised nearly $400 million from investors to help fund over 250 companies.

For Caldbeck, the idea of how to best build a team is important for all people to understand deeply, so it can be articulated to prospective employees, and to help them live more enjoyable lives.

"An ability to identify the passion and express it to others, leads to success and happiness," he says. "I've found over time that my passions were never really about the thing (a sport, investing, technology). They were what that thing gave me, a deep connection with other people, the opportunity to help groups, and the opportunity to impact the world."

Indeed, as we were speaking to people about the ideas in this book, dozens of CEOs agreed with us that enthusiasm is an essential ingredient of hiring. "When evaluating candidates, I'm always trying to determine how passionate they are," says Mike Sweet, CEO of NimblyWise, a company that provides services to prepare students and graduates for continuous learning and success in the knowledge economy. "This signals to me that they are going to proactively learn new things that can help us grow as a company. If this isn't present, I know that I'm going to have to work a lot harder to move the company forward. Given the pace of change in business today, it's a huge handicap if I have to take this on."

Sweet, like Caldbeck, sees a pattern of success.

"In my experience, employees that bring a natural curiosity to what they do are always suggesting new ideas and possibilities and are more resilient when they face challenges," Sweet says. "They'll keep pushing something forward because they are personally invested in it. Their natural enthusiasm is infectious when it comes to getting customers and business partners excited about working with NimblyWise. As they build these external relationships, they are often coming back to the company with ideas for new product innovations. And having strong external relationships is really advantageous in the unfortunate event something goes wrong because it makes difficult conversations a whole lot easier."

Passion can become a habit.

Most employees aren't engaged at work. They're there out of necessity, to draw a paycheck and go home. A tuned-out employee, doing the minimum to get by, is not equipped to help you build your fanocracy.

According to the *State of the Global Workplace* report from Gallup, a company that delivers analytics and advice to help leaders and organizations solve their most pressing problems, only 15 percent of adults who work full time for an employer are highly involved in and enthusiastic about their work and workplace. In the United States the numbers are a little better but still surprisingly low, with 33 percent of employees engaged at work.

Gallup found that these low percentages of engaged employees represent a barrier to creating high-performing cultures around the world. They imply a stunning amount of wasted potential, given that business units in the top quartile of Gallup's global employee engagement database are 17 percent more productive and 21 percent more profitable than those in the bottom quartile.

For the past five years, on an anonymous basis, NimblyWise has worked with Quantum Workplace, an employee engagement software tool, to measure its employees. The NimblyWise numbers have consistently rated way above the Gallup numbers. In the 2017 survey, 97 percent of NimblyWise employees were either highly or moderately engaged, with only 3 percent of employees barely engaged and no employee disengaged.

It turns out that for NimblyWise, hiring passionate employees leads to more engagement at work throughout the organization and directly influences the bottom line. "Our high level of employee engagement helps to drive strong customer satisfaction," Sweet says. "And this translates into our high customer renewal rates which are consistently above 90 percent."

When hiring employees, many CEOs of successful organizations have learned that people are most likely to be evangelistic about a brand if they're evangelistic, period.

HubSpot: Building a Fandom Culture
One Employee at a Time

We looked at how companies hire people who already live a fulfilled life. CEOs of many organizations have learned that hiring passion means the new employees are more likely to be successful. Yet hiring is just the first step in a long relationship with employees. How do you create an organization that cultivates its workforce into fans?

People who feel trusted and are allowed to make their own decisions become passionate about their company.

The key is to build your organizational culture in a way that values each person's decisions about how they show up and contribute. If you allow employees to be themselves, working in the way they find most productive, they are more likely to enjoy their work and therefore become great advocates for the company.

While that may seem easy for a restaurant in Rome with a few dozen staff, it's more difficult in an organization with thousands of employees in offices around the world.

This is why it benefits us to revisit HubSpot, the marketing, sales, and customer service platform company that I wrote about at the beginning of our book. Since my fateful meeting with HubSpot's management team over a decade ago, the company has grown from a handful of employees (remember, *all 10* read my book!) to over 2,000

people. HubSpot is successful by any measure, with more than 60,000 customers paying an average of nearly $10,000 each per year for their HubSpot services.

To drive this success, the company has focused on its corporate culture. In fact, the HubSpot Culture Code, an inside peek at how HubSpot works and what they believe, was published for the world to see on SlideShare and has been viewed nearly four million times. While the 128 slides in the deck provide a remarkable amount of detail, HubSpot summarizes its Culture Code as these attributes:

1. Culture is to recruiting as product is to marketing.
2. Whether you like it or not, you're going to have a culture. Why not make it one you love?
3. Solve for the Customer—not just their happiness, but also their success.
4. Power is now gained by sharing knowledge, not hoarding it.
5. "Sunlight is the best disinfectant."
6. You shouldn't penalize the many for the mistakes of the few.
7. Results should matter more than when or where they are produced.
8. Influence should be independent of hierarchy.
9. Great people want direction on where they're going—not directions on how to get there.
10. "Better a diamond with a flaw than a pebble without."
11. We'd rather be failing frequently than never trying.

"We are building a company that our employees truly love," Katie Burke, the chief people officer at HubSpot, told us. "It starts with believing that our employees can and should love their work so we're

doing our best to be as remarkable with the value proposition we create for our *employees* as what we do for our *customers*."

Two important drivers of the HubSpot culture are the focus on autonomy and transparency. "My hope for every HubSpotter when they work here is not just that they become better engineers or marketers, but that they ideally become better people and better professionals and better entrepreneurs," Burke says. "To do that they need access to information they wouldn't normally have as part of their job. For me it's a great source of pride that people who just started on their team as interns can read wiki posts from cofounders Brian and Dharmesh on what they're thinking about business strategy. That is a really powerful force of learning."

This kind of openness and transparency is sometimes difficult for executives who are used to a traditional hierarchical, command-and-control management style. "You have to be transparent when it's not convenient for you," Burke says. "You have to be transparent even when it feels difficult. It's something we all hold each other accountable to."

What I find remarkable is that HubSpot's culture includes an unlimited-vacation policy. Employees can take as much vacation as they need. Who else does that? "We have employees who sometimes work long hours," Burke says. "We hire great people, and one of our principles is autonomy, so why would we have them sign a permission slip to take vacation time? They're adults and it makes no sense. Our cofounders are both allergic to policies that are nonsensical, and that's baked into our culture. We want people to be in the driver's seat of their own lives and careers and so the ultimate goal is for people to build their work around their life, not the other way around."

It's proved to be a very successful approach. HubSpot was voted by its employees as one of the top ten best places to work in 2018, winning a Glassdoor Employees' Choice Award in the large companies category. The award recognizes the best workplaces and company cultures based on employee reviews and feedback via Glassdoor, one of the largest and fastest-growing job sites. Other top ten places to work included Facebook, Google, and Netflix. At the time of the announcement, HubSpot had 547 employee reviews, and an overall rating of 4.7 out of 5.

On Glassdoor, current and former employees of companies worldwide can share insights and opinions about their work environments by writing a review about their company. The reviews on the site are designed to give the reader an insider's look at what it's like to work at particular jobs and companies. People considering taking a job with HubSpot study these reviews, and many potential customers and investors check them out as well. Here are examples of what HubSpot employees say about the company on Glassdoor:

I'm surrounded all day by brilliant, thoughtful, and ambitious people. Collaboration and ideas from the very bottom of the chain is not only accepted but highly encouraged—I've always felt like HubSpot genuinely values my ideas and seeks them. Every day I am challenged to learn new skills and continue growing with the company.

—Employee on the Customer Success team

I started at HubSpot with limited sales experience, but a love for the Inbound mission and a relentless desire to contribute however I could. I did my day job well, took on new challenges, and no one ever told me no or to slow down. Instead, my colleagues taught me more, and pushed me to continue to improve. Nearly 5 years later I am in a key leadership role in sales and have elevated my career beyond my wildest dreams. I love HubSpot. There is an ever thriving startup culture even as the company scales, and I get an opportunity to learn from and be challenged by incredible people every single day.

—Employee on the Sales team

Absolutely awesome culture—yes the perks are fantastic (on-site barista, on-site gym, free snacks, unlimited PTO, etc) but the people, the transparency, the value on the employees and building teamwork, and arming employees with the tools to make them successful are just a few reasons why people love working here. I've worked in a number of companies up to this point, and I've never felt more like a company actually values me and my contribution than they do here.

—Anonymous employee

Based on these reviews and hundreds of others like them, it's clear that HubSpot has already created a fanocracy among its employees, who are happy to share their enthusiasm with the world.

"When CEOs of other companies ask me about our Glassdoor rating, they ask about the wrong thing," Burke says. "They want to know how do you get that rating? They think it's about is how you market to employees and ask them to write a review. But I tell them it starts with thinking of your employee experience as a product unto itself. The ranking is a lagging indicator of what we're doing. Not a leading indicator of what we're doing. And so, if you're focused on just the rankings and reviews, you're doing it wrong. All day, all I think about is how we are innovating to keep up with what our employees expect from us.

How are we responding to their feedback? How do we make sure we're taking it to the next level every single year? When we win an award, the next morning I think about what are we going to do *next* year? Just like building any great product, complacency is the ultimate enemy."

HubSpot has enthusiastic employees who write glowing reviews of what it's like to work at the company, and that helps win awards. So how do those employee fans work to make the company a financial success? How does this build a fanocracy?

"Part of our culture code is to solve for the customer and people know that coming in," Burke says. "So if you're someone who doesn't care or just wants to build for the sake of building, you're probably not going to join HubSpot. If you do join HubSpot you're starting with a product team that cares deeply about customer feedback and spends a lot of time listening to customers and partners about what's working and what isn't. Chances are you want the autonomy to be able to fix problems. We have really small autonomous teams on our product organization to give them flexibility to make decisions to solve for our customers on a regular basis."

In a world where people have come to expect poor customer service and aggressive sales tactics, HubSpot people focus on what's best for customers, not what's going to bring in a deal faster or save money. "Our customer support people are given full autonomy to help solve the actual issue that somebody is dealing with versus trying to put them on hold for as long as possible to delay and prevent them from actually getting the help they need," Burke says.

The annual HubSpot INBOUND conference draws tens of thousands of fans from all over the world to Boston each year to learn more about effective marketing, sales, and customer support strategies. Yet most come to interact with people who work at HubSpot and meet their loyal clients. Speakers such as Michelle Obama, John Cena, Seth

Godin, Brené Brown, and Martha Stewart have given keynote presentations. The weeklong event features almost three hundred breakout sessions.

People get so much out of the event that they dedicate nearly a week of their time, gladly investing in the event ticket, air travel, and hotel accommodations. They say it's worth it to have the chance to interact with HubSpot people.

"I have yet to meet someone for whom meeting a HubSpot person did not make them more likely to buy our product or more likely to attend a HubSpot user group meeting or more likely to come to our INBOUND conference," Burke says. "That's a sign we're doing something right. And we hear time and time again that one of the reasons people bet on us is our people. They believe that the professional that they dealt with as part of their sales process was highly consultative and helpful. I have never worked at a software company besides HubSpot where someone has said, 'I absolutely love my sales rep and I want to stay in touch with them.' That's a point of pride."

Earlier I mentioned Pete Cipollone, coxswain of the world-record-setting 2004 Athens Olympic gold medal US men's eight rowing team, who is now CEO of InstaViser. As an athlete and as a CEO, Cipollone is a leader who channels the passions of his teams. The final moments of his race call, the 1997 Head of the Charles where his team broke the course record, played out like this:

Guys, three hundred fifty meters to go, now drive.
Legs, cleaner, cleaner.
Drive with power, sit up taller, sit up taller.
In two we go again.

It might be close, get ready!

One sit up.

Up NOW!

Two hundred and fifty, two hundred and fifty to go, go now!

Push, chaaa.

Push, chaaa.

Push, chaaa.

Last twenty strokes, go, NOW!

Legs!

Legs!

Legs!

Legs!

Good, go for it!

[cheers come up from finish line area] Now!

Push, chaaa.

Push, chaaa.

Push, chaaa.

Legs, last five, go!

One.

Two.

Three.

Fo'

Easy!

Good piece, keep rowing.

PART III

Enjoying Fanocracy

CHAPTER 13

A Passionate Life

by Reiko

I t was 6:00 a.m. and there were three of us packed into a tiny room in a New York City hostel. Black skirts, mesh shirts, hair curlers, and jewelry were strewn across the twin beds as we crowded around the single mirror, taking turns applying each other's makeup. I closed my eyes as I let my friend draw streaks of black over my eyelids and cheeks. I scrunched up my nose, the unfamiliar feeling of face paint crinkling across my skin.

"So, Claire, how does it look?" I asked her, my fingers itching to touch her drying work. Claire looked back at me, eyes bright behind the matching dark streaks of makeup sweeping across her face.

"Good," she said, slapping my hand away from my face. "Now stop touching it, or you'll mess it up."

I withdrew my arm and my laugh pulled at my lipstick. "You're going to have to keep reminding me," I said.

I peeked at my reflection in the mirror as I pulled out my phone and held it up to see a drawing from a panel of the comic book series The Wicked + The Divine by Kieron Gillen and Jamie McKelvie. She had captured perfectly the sharp lines of the markings, from nose to hairline, of the character I was trying to portray. I tried a scowl, matching the expression on the comic panel. I could hardly recognize myself. The transformation was coming together.

"That's enough admiring yourself," the third in our group, Jenny, said. "Help me with my corset."

Jenny, Claire, and I share a similar taste in books and comics, often trading recommendations or borrowing from one another's shelves so we can talk about them together over dinner. The Wicked + The Divine was one of the many the three of us have passed around, a series we love for its beautiful art and multilayered plot about reincarnations of ancient gods who earn their contemporary fame as pop singers. That day, we were dressing up as one of the characters, the Morrigan, Celtic goddess of war. She has three forms and we each chose one to portray: Macha (Claire, with black hair and black clothes, she's the steadiest form of the three), Gentle Annie (Jenny, bald and kind, the whimsical form), and Badb (me, with flaming and wild hair, the form that holds Morrigan's anger).

From arranging black feathers across our shoulders and doing our hair, the three of us looked a terror together—carefully painted birds twisting up each of our arms, black witchlike dresses, and my hair hidden away under a bright red wig that extended down my back to my hips. As we left our rooms to catch an Uber, it was still early, and the street was not yet crowded with tourists or shoppers. Still, we got a few curious stares before the car drove up.

Our driver raised one eyebrow as we jumped into the back.

"Costume party?" he asked.

A costume party? A simple costume party wouldn't have taken months of planning and the stress of squeezing in a trip to another city during my busy medical school schedule.

"Comic Con," Jenny told the driver.

Comic Con: Embracing My Fandom Pride

It was my fifth year in a row going to New York City Comic Con at the Javits convention center. This was the same Con where I had met the author Ngozi Ukazu several years before, as well as many other authors and artists and actors I admired. It was something I looked forward to for months, sitting through my classes or spending long hours at work dreaming about this early weekend in October.

Jenny, Claire, and I had gone to college together in New York City, and we had all moved to Boston after graduation. We stayed in touch, growing even closer than we had been in school through our similar tastes in books and comics. Our connection to New York and its community of fans had never left us, though, and every year we made the trip back to Comic Con.

As we drew closer to the Javits Center, the sidewalk became more and more filled with vibrant colors from the gathering of costumed people. We were three of nearly two hundred thousand attendees visiting from all over the country for cosplay and panels and meet-and-greets with creators and fellow fans.

"Good luck," our driver said as he dropped us off.

"I'll need it," I called back as I pulled my long skirt behind me and I climbed out, thinking about how I'd need luck today not to trip over myself.

As he drove away, I thought back to how my friends and I planned this experience for months and loved doing so. Though we spent hours that morning getting ready, the real work had happened long before we got on a bus to the city. We'd sent each other links for fabric or techniques for sewing and snapped photos of any progress we had made. Yet as we entered the sea of attendees, I felt self-conscious that our costumes wouldn't be good enough, we wouldn't be recognizable, or I'd smear my makeup when I drank some water. What would I say to the creators of The Wicked + The Divine when we finally met them? What would they say to us? Was I wasting my valuable time on make-believe?

Swallowed by the crowd, we were quickly mixed in with six-foot-long foam swords, pointed hats, and shining armor. "I love your cloak. How did you make it?" I overheard to my left. "Did you see the giveaway Image has today?" another voice said. "I'm heading to the Dark Horse booth first. I want to make sure they don't run out of those posters." I looked around at other people's costumes, and some I recognized from the works I enjoy and some I didn't. No one shouted out our character names like they did for those who turned and waved to a passing Loki, Korra, or Zelda.

My stomach was in my throat as my friends and I headed to Artist Alley in the lower levels of the Javits Center, where we knew the creators of The Wicked + The Divine would be. After waiting in line, comics in our hands ready for their signatures, we finally arrived in front of them. But before we could speak, they clapped wildly and laughed and said, "Amazing!"

And before we could ask for a picture with them, *they* asked for a picture of *us*.

"This is going up on my Instagram," cheered Jamie McKelvie. "Your costumes look great!"

I grinned. I hadn't ever imagined these creators would be as excited to see *us* as *we* were *them*. That was the moment I remembered why I loved it here. I was a teenager again, eager, giddy, and loud. And our enthusiasm was welcomed. What I had forgotten is how much love fuels the art that we enjoy. The spark of our excitement was contagious.

On that Saturday morning in New York City, I wasn't wasting my time. I was having the time of my life with my friends, interacting with the creative people I admired.

Creating a Common Language of Connection

Have you noticed how it becomes too easy to slip into hours or days behind a computer without taking time for a real conversation with friends? Do we delude ourselves that seeing updates on Twitter are the same as checking in with our loved ones? Is a comment on Facebook the same as having a coffee with a friend? When was the last time you said, "I heard Paul got married," but you never actually heard anyone say it, and instead realized you meant you saw a photo of Paul during his honeymoon in Costa Rica on Instagram?

We've become so used to being one click away from sending a message that we only scratch the surface of friendship. We forget what it is that brought us together with our friends in the first place. We dig ourselves into ever-deeper holes of isolation or loneliness. We rely on things like social media platforms to form a virtual replacement and write messages to our friends, but based on how compulsively we check to see if we've gotten a response, we want more.

Don't you want more than rushed chats when you reach out to old friends? Isn't there more to life than the shallow office talk we schmooze through when we're concerned about being "professional"? When did being professional replace being yourself?

Instead of two people who used to know each other struggling to find a reason to say hello, we soon become two people who get together every week to watch a favorite sitcom. It can be the first step to having a real connection when coworkers realize that they cheer for the same college football team—or the start of a string of teasing texts when they realize they cheer for rival teams.

It is a way to say to the world: "This is who I am. This is what I love. Please, join me in this joy."

Fandom begins with the creation of a common language that allows us to connect.

Many of us worry that pouring our hearts into the activities we love will affect how others see us. That somehow it will cloud our judgment and turn us into those clueless fanatics we so often hear about—the gamer in his basement, or the brainless screaming sports fan. Fandom, for some people, is relegated as escapism, deemed childish or a waste of time. Not something for "professionals." For a long time, I was hesitant to share what I liked because I was self-conscious about how I might be perceived.

It took effort and courage for my friends and me to dress up as the Morrigan, yet when we did, we found that we weren't putting on another persona. Rather, we were reflecting a part of ourselves that we couldn't show any other way. For me, it was a way for me to be true, authentic—more so than I could ever be on the curated version of myself I post online. I enjoyed myself more, and I felt I could inspire enthusiasm in others. Jamie McKelvie saw the work we put into our cosplay and couldn't wait to share his excitement with *his* followers on social media. Our outpouring of our passions didn't go unnoticed.

Perhaps even more significantly, while I'd done cosplay before, it was my first year in a group costume. The fandom I'd shared with my friends tied us together, just as our love for the life of a fan tied us to other attendees dressed as their favorite characters.

All of these things amount to a common language of fanocracy. It is the understanding of *you*, as an individual and as part of a group.

And isn't that what you want with your friends? With your colleagues? With your customers? With the people you want to work with in organizations or as collaborators? Isn't the ability to share a vast range of experiences—activities and obsessions people have devoted their time and energy to—an exquisitely *positive* thing? Isn't that also what you want for yourself?

If you hide that thing within you that drives you to dive deep into what you love and enjoy it with your full being—that spark—nobody will see you at your truest self. On the other hand, when we engage ourselves fully in our fandoms, that spark will ignite inside us and spread to others.

Fandom is not wish fulfillment or escapism. It isn't about work-life balance or a mindless activity just to relax. Instead, it's a way that more and more people can solve a fundamental problem of isolation. It is what the most engaged and fulfilled people do to enhance their lives. You can see it in their behavior: they seem to laugh and smile more, joke about their mistakes, take life lightly, and enjoy themselves.

> **Successful people understand that to ignite a spark in another, they must first ignite that spark in themselves.**

In our interviews with hundreds of fans—enthusiasts of things as diverse as skiing and triathlons, knitting and painting, flamenco guitar and a capella singing, classic cars and RVs—it's abundantly clear to us that those people who build their personal passions into their lives are able to see the world in a different light. They live a truer life by expressing themselves through their fandoms. They pull energy, new ideas, and deep connections from and then back to like-minded people. They learn valuable lessons from their fandoms that they can't learn anywhere else, whether that be humor, empathy, or creativity.

Fanocracy isn't just for our clients or our businesses. It is a state of mind we can value in ourselves. Through stories of a young archeologist turned businesswoman to a concertgoer turned activist, we will see that redefining our identities around what we love is key to being able to rally others to our cause.

Jimi Hendrix Fans at a Flamenco Concert

Music is a way we learn to express ourselves growing up—first by listening to our parents' music, then perhaps radio or television or venturing out and finding artists and genres that vibe with us. Because of that, listening to a familiar song can be a powerful force of nostalgia that binds us, emotionally, to the memory of a time, place, or group of people we knew then.

Juanito Pascual, flamenco guitarist, composer, and touring musician, understands this well. He was twelve years old, the age we build our personal identities, when he started formal guitar lessons, and also twelve years old when he started listening to bands that would define his fandoms well into his professional career. He realized quickly that to build a relationship with his listeners, he had to make them personally invested in some way.

"In my early twenties I became aware that my fandom was broad but particular. Everything from the Grateful Dead to flamenco, of course, and jazz and Latin music," Pascual told us. "But if I was doing any one of those things at any one time, all of the other fan bases would be completely unaware of me. If I'm playing flamenco, the average Grateful Dead fan is not going to have any idea." As a fan, Pascual is very aware of how his own range of fandoms influence the musical work he does. Though his core genre is flamenco, he finds that an essential piece in his communication onstage with his audiences around the world is his ability to cross boundaries musically, incorporating the artists he loves most—the musicians he grew up listening to when he was figuring out his identity as a guitarist—into each of his performances.

At a show, he may pick up his guitar and play a cover of Jimi Hendrix in a flamenco style, and he gains fans he wouldn't normally have. When he improvises onstage—something uncommon in flamenco performance culture—he's paying homage to both the jazz and jam band genres he grew up listening to. He can play the first few lines of "While My Guitar Gently Weeps" by the Beatles and there's an instant connection when the audience starts to clap. "It lets them know I'm one of them," Pascual says, describing how he's an active participant in the music community as both a fan and an artist. "If those people that I'm in a group of fans with knew about what I'm doing as a flamenco artist, they may see the connection and enjoy what I'm doing as well."

Many musicians, including flamenco artists, have varied influences, yet none have the specific set that Pascual has because it is a mix of what he heard as a child and the music that inspired him when he performed. His passion for other genres makes his music better and allows him to be creative in a way unique to his experience. His music has become a reflection of his life story, but the way he shares it allows him to build a relationship with his audience.

What about you? Almost everyone reading this, I assume, will be well past twelve years old, yet you may not have something to call *your* fandom . . . yet. Perhaps you simply haven't clicked with anything in particular. That doesn't mean that fandom isn't for you. While the age of puberty is one in which many people establish fandoms that stay with them for life, we met plenty of people who discovered their passions later, some even into their retirement years.

It may just be that you haven't yet found that one activity that sparks your interest. It also may be that you *do* have a skill or a hobby or an obsession that you didn't realize could be a bigger part of your life than it is now. Perhaps you never thought to think of yourself as a fan. Maybe you simply don't know other people that are obsessed by the same thing as you are.

> **Adolescence wasn't the end of your fandom journey, it was only the beginning.**

Many times, it takes a reigniting of a flame that has been smoldering since you were young. Think back to what you couldn't stop talking about when you were reaching your teen years—what your parents couldn't pry you away from, or what you saved your summer job money to buy. Is there some way to connect back to that excitement? Is there any equivalent you can find in your life now that could give you the same joy? And how can you put yourself into proximity with other people who share the same interests? What have you been putting off until you "have the time"?

There are many ways to consciously build your engaged identity, regardless of when you might have developed a fandom, or if you are currently in the process of finding what feels right. From an old loved activity that becomes a career to a hobby that just won't go away, there are infinite ways to weave our own passions into our lives to be more successful and happier in the work we do.

When You Are a Fan of What You Do

I was recently chatting with my friend Jenny, one of the Morrigan characters in our group of three at Comic Con. Now, instead of being among the crowds at the convention center, we were in my dining room, sipping wine in our casual sweaters and jeans instead of corsets and face paint. In her professional life, she is an editorial associate at a major publishing house that works in everything from fiction to memoir to field guides. Jenny focuses on the company's poetry collection, supporting authors to put their work out into the world, as well as discovering new poets to publish. For Jenny, her professional life and her personal love of books overlap.

"In the publishing house itself, the editor is the number one fan for the author," Jenny said, explaining how she uses her excitement about an author both as a gauge to assess how well they'll do in the market and as fuel to push her work. "Another word we sometimes use is 'cheerleader' or 'champion.' It's really cheesy, but it's true. You're the entry to the company, getting everyone in the company excited about it. That's supposed to be reflective of and an opportunity to transmit beyond the company. So if everyone's excited, you can think, *Oh, I think I have something good on my hands.*"

Jenny has been engrossed with the literary world since she was young—a love of books leading to a career in the industry. The simple act of loving a great book had shaped her to be the most effective person for her job. She leveraged the identity she forged over time to make her livelihood. When she talks about what stories she's adored, I can tell that her passion fuels her work and vice versa. The energy that she both gives and receives is the key to her work in publishing.

Marrying her work to her passion has only strengthened the love Jenny kindled when she was young. What she is reading for work influences what she wants to read at home. "I got into graphic novels because of work. I was interviewing and saw my boss worked on Alison Bechdel, so I checked her out. And I loved it and was obsessed with it. That got me started on graphic novels and comics, something I never realized I would be a fan of, never having read it growing up." What she reads in her own time also makes her think about what could be possible to introduce to the marketplace. "After I started watching K dramas, I thought about it in terms of my work. K dramas are so popular and people in America love them so much. Surely there must be something we can do in terms of the literary scene." Even if her fandom is older, she keeps finding new things to become passionate about. New ideas that allow her to grow in both professional taste and pleasure.

The best person at any job is the person who loves it the most.

"It's the community where everyone is obsessed with the larger idea of storytelling," she said, smiling to herself. "That's a fandom in itself. Can we call it that? There are movie buffs and then there are us, bookworms."

I laughed and agreed. "Bookworms" sounded right.

As an editor, she relies on her ability to discern what literature will be successful, trusting taste by how excited it makes her. It is her ability to *share* that excitement with others that makes her both a fan and good editor. "I like what I like, but I'm always willing to be surprised," she said. "I'm always ready to be a fan of something and use that fandom to make other people fans. Isn't that what everybody wants? A bigger fandom?"

That passion is what drives her—and it is the very same passion that drew me to her as a friend—trusting her word when she passed me each new story to read and discuss over potluck dinners. I can see that she doesn't simply like something passively, but rather throws her whole being into her interests, because that is what satisfies her and creates results.

Indeed, the simplest way to connect your identity to your professional life is to make it one and the same. When you can fuel the fandom you love by pouring your energy into it, you end up making it a better place for everyone around you—at work and at home.

The Girl Who Found a Dinosaur

Not all of our interests and fandoms are steady and unwavering from childhood like Jenny's. Sometimes, we take journeys of obsession and move on, or pick up a new hobby later in life. That doesn't mean that we can't learn from those past experiences. Often, it is the journey itself, throwing ourselves so fully into one subject, that leads us to understand where we want to go next. To understand where our passions will be best utilized.

This is what the girl who found a dinosaur realized when she grew up. India Wood, who had uncovered the most complete allosaurus

ever found at just twelve years old, didn't grow up to become a paleontologist. Instead, she built her own company, Hart Business Research,
to analyze various creative markets including needle arts, knitting,
painting, drawing, and sculpture.

"I was twelve years old and had gone out with my sister and a ranch
hand to hunt for fossils," Wood says, telling a story about her childhood in rural Colorado in the late 1970s. "They walked a lot faster than
I did and I found myself alone. I noticed a little piece of bone sticking
out of the hill so I started to dig that. After an hour or two my sister
showed up with the ranch hand and they helped me dig. I was just having fun! I had no idea when I found it whether it was just one little piece
of bone or an entire dinosaur. But once I started to dig, it was like a slot
machine. It started off giving me a penny when I found that little piece
of bone. Then it clanked out a quarter, some good-sized pieces. Then I
dug all the way back into the hill and found an entire bone. Man, the
slot machine just gave me a thousand bucks!"

At the time she found her first bone, twelve-year-old Wood was
fascinated by Charles Darwin and by women scientists, but the few
pictures she had seen of dinosaur hunters in *National Geographic*
showed them as trained adults equipped with proper tools. At less than
five feet tall and just seventy-five pounds, and using an old hammer
and screwdriver to dig, she felt completely unqualified.

It was the thrill of discovery, her obsession with finding more, and
the sense of accomplishment when she did, that kept her going. Over
the course of three years, she came back to that spot again and again,
uncovering fossil after fossil, hiding the dozens of bones under her bed
or in her bedroom closet. When she wasn't in the field, she read about
paleontology. From a book borrowed from her junior high school
teacher, she was able to identify one of the 150-million-year old bones
she found as part of an allosaurus pelvis.

"It was an escape from problems at home too," Wood said, joking that the dinosaur raised her more than her parents did. "I was excited about being sucked into the world of this particular dinosaur out in the desert, but it was also this tremendous refuge. Finding the allosaurus gave me a particular thing to really home in on."

Eventually, when her mother grew tired of the allosaurus littering her bedroom, Wood took a few of the bones to the Denver Museum of Nature and Science to see if her identification was correct. The museum's paleontologist quickly told her that her incredible discovery was indeed an allosaurus. The museum hired young Wood, and together she and the professional paleontologists worked for another year to finish excavating what would become the most complete allosaurus ever found. Alice, as Wood affectionately refers to her dinosaur, ended up being profiled together with Wood on television, on radio, and in magazines and newspapers, and is visited at the Denver Museum of Nature and Science by 1.7 million people every year. India Wood became known as "the Girl Who Found a Dinosaur."

To many people's surprise, however, the girl who found a dinosaur moved on from her amazing find and chose a different path as an adult. What Wood took from her childhood wasn't the *object* of her passion, but rather her knowledge of how passion itself works—the very details and nuances of what makes people obsessed and coming back for more, just like she did with her dinosaur. So she founded her company, Hart Business Research, to study just that: what makes people love their art? Sponsored by the National Arts Association, Wood's company surveys tens of thousands of artists to look at the details of their passion, from what emotions they experience when they are knitting to reasons artists buy a particular brand of paint. That data then helps independent retailers and family businesses compete with Amazon or Costco by informing them of how best to reach their customers.

"What it comes down to is creative people like to create because it makes them feel happy, relaxed, and accomplished," Wood says about her data. That holds true for all people, inside or outside creative industries.

"I dug up the allosaurus because it made me feel accomplished. I felt joy out there in nature," she says. "I was also passionate about producing studies of creative industries because it made me feel accomplished."

It was the emotions she experienced when she was doing something she loved—the joy she felt as the dinosaur bones piled up under her bed—that allowed her to move on and create a company dedicated to studying when others felt the same way. And through the data she gathered, she was able to help many other small businesses succeed.

The Sheer Delight in Other People's Passions

Fandom is a training in passion of all types. Not only does it inform a way forward in career, as it did with India Wood, but continued interest in activities outside work can serve as a continuous resource for joy and inspiration that will spill over into work life. The dedication one person feels outside work can translate to dedication in a company, even if the subject is completely different.

That is what Rebecca Corliss understands very well. She is vice president of marketing at Owl Labs, a startup creating new video conferencing technology to allow remote workers to be more effective participants in their company's meetings, no matter where they are located.

And what is Corliss passionate about? A capella. As she says, "I used to say I went to college to be in an a capella group and took classes on the side. It was very identity-forming for me."

She sang from the time she was young, through college, and after graduating as a working adult, went on to form two a capella groups, becoming a self-described "acapreneur." Since her sophomore year of college until now, into her thirties, she has always been in an a capella group, constantly going to competitions, performing gigs, and recording.

Corliss laughs and adds, "You really have to love something to put in *that* much work. I can't imagine a world in which I'm not singing. If I'm not singing, I'm not whole or happy. As a happier person, I can do more, be more effective in everything I do."

Corliss understands that this feeling is within all the successful people she has ever worked with, so when hiring, she focuses on finding people who love things outside work. For example, when she interviews potential employees, the question she loves to ask is this: "If you walked into a gymnasium filled with two thousand totally random people, what could you confidently say you are better at than everyone?"

The answers vary, but what she is most interested in is not the subject but the opportunity to very naturally draw out each person's obsession. One answer was Rubik's cube: an interviewee talked excitedly about how he had learned the combinations to solve anything in under forty-five seconds. "You see these people light up," Corliss says. "That's amazing. That means you're inspired with the job you're interviewing for. When you light up, you'll do amazing things."

"I will go as far as I need, to make a capella be successful for me. That's something I can also tap into when I'm working. When I'm inspired, I can go as far as I need to," Corliss says, citing her ability to build multiple a capella groups from scratch because she wanted to sing. "Identifying people who have a passion, no matter what it may be, really gives an upper hand in the workplace. If you are someone who can be inspired, and especially to an intense degree, I know you are the type of person who will go above and beyond to make something happen."

It is these workers who *do* light up and *do* talk about their other obsessions whom Corliss identified as the most forward thinking. These are the ones who are never satisfied with what has already been accomplished but are motivated to see what is next. Passionate people, Corliss says, are excited about the future. And that is what is best for any company.

HeadCount: Musicians for Democracy

The energy that fans create can be massive and powerful. It can move beyond the individual, beyond the company, and beyond the context of its origin. The roar of a crowd at a concert doesn't need to quiet when the lights go up. It can expand. It can spread. That kind of energy can go on to be a resource for altruism, philanthropy, and activism.

Consider an organization founded to take the enormous energy of music fandom and channel that into registering people to vote in the United States. HeadCount, a nonpartisan organization, works with musicians to reach their fans to promote participation in democracy. It stages voter registration drives by setting up booths at concerts including those of St. Vincent, Maroon 5, Harry Styles, and Drake. It also taps into musicians' fandoms on social media, asking artists to be in a photograph where they hold up a sign that simply says VOTE or I VOTE BECAUSE _____, with the artist filling in the blank. The artist then shares their photo on their social media channels, reaching their fans. More than five hundred artists have participated in these social media outreach programs, including Jack Johnson, "Weird Al" Yankovic, Killer Mike, Ani DiFranco, Questlove, Lil Dicky, and Amanda Palmer, and members of bands including Kings of Leon, Guster, Disco Biscuits, Dispatch, and many others.

By reaching music fans where they already are, at concerts and on-line, HeadCount has registered more than a half million voters in the United States since 2004 and has built a huge network of twenty thousand volunteers nationwide.

The key to the success of HeadCount is the ability to tap into music fans where the collective energy is high—at concerts. "There's a very simple idea behind HeadCount that musicians are leaders. They have this platform to reach a lot of people and that's a great way to engage people around the electoral process and civic participation," Andy Bernstein, executive director of HeadCount, told us. "But I'd say the real secret sauce is community and that's when you get into a true fandom. The reason that people get involved to begin with is because of their love of music, and even more so of their love of the music community, and finally, the enjoyment of meeting like-minded people through music. HeadCount becomes a way for you to get deeper into that community, give back to that community and become engaged citizens. You become real leaders, not just voters, but a person who leads other people to vote. That's the dynamic that we have leveraged. The community element of fandom drives us."

Fans are already excited about the artists they love, and when HeadCount shows that these artists feel that participating in US democracy is vitally important to them, that passion translates. The spark spreads, and these fans now have an emotional drive, not just an intellectual incentive, to vote.

Another example of the powerful good that fandoms can generate is the nonprofit organization the Harry Potter Alliance (HPA), founded in 2005 by comedian Andrew Slack. Slack and his band, Harry and the Potters, a rock group that combines comedy, music, and the fandom of the Harry Potter universe, had started by collecting donations at their concerts for Amnesty International to draw attention to human rights violations in Sudan. Since then, the HPA has grown and engaged millions of fans in campaigns, including those for literacy, mental health, economic justice, US immigration reform, and more. Some of their successes include raising over $123,000 for Partners In Health to send five cargo planes of life-saving supplies to Haiti and donating over 390,000 books across the world through their Accio Books campaign. The HPA was able to channel the younger voices in fandom that would otherwise be unheard into a united front, transforming the moral lessons in the books into real-world change.

Tapping into fanocracies that have already been built by hundreds of musicians or bookworms has proven to be a great way to encourage people to participate in civic service. It is translating a passion that already exists in a different form and directing it toward a cause. When fans see their community excited about something, no matter how close or far to the original uniting factor of that fandom, the excitement is infectious.

The spark can turn into a flame and, as the HPA writes on its website, the organization "turns fans into heroes."

The Secret Language of Passionate People

Back at New York Comic Con with my friends, halfway through the day, the three of us still fully costumed as the Morrigan and dragging our ever-enlarging bags of prized merchandise, we went to a panel on women of color breaking into the publishing industry. The panel was made up of a range of women from comic writers to marketers, and was moderated by a young woman rocking a full costume of the Chinese American X-Men hero, Jubilee.

After the session ended, I began to reflect on what I thought about the discussion and tried to dig my schedule out of my bag to figure out where we were heading next. But Jenny peeled off to approach the table on the stage, joining a handful of others doing the same, some to shake hands with an author they were a fan of, or to ask a question they didn't get to during the session.

But for Jenny, it was something more. Jenny is an editor, and so was the moderator. They already knew each other as colleagues.

The scene of the two of them talking shop while dressed as comic book characters, Jenny in her black and mesh and the moderator in the iconic yellow jacket of Jubilee, wasn't as jarring as I would have first thought. They were laughing and chatting and looking like many other fans passing by us in the hall. They were on equal ground, fully immersed in this intersecting world of professional and personal, committed to how they wanted to express their own connections to fandom. They were proud comic book lovers, experiencing the Con from the perspective of anyone else on the floor. They were also in the industry, eager to make connections that could not only enhance their own careers but also make the publishing world somewhere that fans like them would feel at home.

What Jenny and her colleague had was an understanding of each other and a trust that they both loved the thing they worked on. In a basement hall of a convention center, cosplaying and showing their fandom surrounded by many other excited fans, these two literary professionals were much closer to the energy of what drives their work than they would have been if they were stuck ten stories up in a cubicle-laden corporate office.

This is what our fandoms do—they bring us closer to one another so that we may share our joy with others. They are a way to communicate who we are. More than that, they make us happy.

And with that happiness, we find the energy to do extraordinary work.

CHAPTER 14

Share Your Fandom

by David & Reiko

Many people have been surprised to learn that we've worked together on this project. "A father and daughter writing a book together? What's up with that?" they ask. The spark of the idea came when we realized how similar our ideas of fandoms are, yet how different we are as people. Both of our lives have been greatly influenced by the things that we love, and the people who share our passions are among our best friends. Because we had the same strong feelings about the importance of fandom in our lives, we appreciated that we had identified something important and worth exploring together.

Fandom is neither a weakness nor a distraction. To love things outside work fosters a meaningful connection with other like-minded people. This connection provides a richer and more fulfilling life. In our case, our shared love of live music has brought us together in a powerful way, father and daughter bonding at concerts. Similarly, David and Yukari share a love of interesting travel and great food while Reiko and her husband, Ben, can't wait to play games like Magic: The Gathering together. Shared fandom builds a fanocracy at home as much as at work.

As we were working on final edits to the last chapter of *Fanocracy*, we both simultaneously received an identical email. David was on a train returning home from a meeting, and Reiko was at a hospital between seeing patients. We both immediately opened the email message on our smartphones. The subject line was "2019 Lineup | Announce Day" and it came from the Boston Calling music festival. We each scanned the dozens of bands just announced to play the festival, looking for old favorites, pausing on several we hadn't seen live but were eager to check out (Greta Van Fleet for David, Janelle Monáe for Reiko). And then we quickly messaged each other with excitement, sharing our picks. We had been to three other Boston Calling music festivals together and always looked forward to being in the warm sunshine sharing our mutual love of live music.

A fanocracy results from making business personal.

As we've said, a fanocracy is a blueprint for bringing friends and family together to celebrate what they love. For us, live music was our catalyst to a remarkably strong relationship. It also kept us together through a shared language despite any distance that separated us.

We're excited that each of us has the power to develop a similarly strong relationship with our family members, friends, colleagues, and clients as we share what we are passionate about.

We want to personally thank you, our readers, for being a part of this journey with us. At our website, www.fanocracy.com, you will find our fanocracy stories video channel that includes examples of many people who have created a fanocracy, our interviews with nearly twenty of the 2020 US presidential candidates on what they are most passionate about, and presentations we've delivered on the topic of fanocracy. We also invite you to download our "Nine Steps to Building a Fanocracy in Your Business" checklist infographic designed to help you implement the ideas of this book in your business. Visit www.fanocracy.com /resources, and use the passcode FanocracyNow to download. As the ideas of fanocracy evolve with your help, we hope to share much more on the site.

The years researching and writing this book have been a defining part of our lives and have brought us much closer together. We're confident that developing a similar passion in your life will do the same for you, bringing you closer to your customers, your friends, and your family.

Because you will create your longest-lasting relationship—in both your personal and professional life—when you share your fandom.

ACKNOWLEDGMENTS

The spark for this book occurred more than five years ago as we realized that our ideas about fans and fandom were strikingly similar, yet as people we are so utterly different. Over meals, while driving in the car, and via email, we discussed and debated. We quickly realized that we needed to share our thoughts, and this book was born. Since then, many people have helped us along the way as we've gone from random ideas to the finished book. We've spoken to hundreds of people about their fandoms, and we want to thank them all.

Our agent, Margret McBride, was the first to grasp that a jumble of concepts could be turned into a coherent narrative. Even more than shepherding us through the publishing process with skill and humor, she helped us craft *Fanocracy* into a complete set of ideas. Margret went far beyond her job as an agent and became our knowledgeable consultant, master of language, tireless cheerleader, and friend. We thank her for all the long days and endless emails and phone calls that made this book what it is. Margret's colleague Faye Atchison was instrumental in keeping us on track and making sure that our wild ideas were grounded in reality. Thank you, Margret and Faye!

At Portfolio, we are indebted to Will Weisser, who saw something in our ideas and took a chance on working with us. Will and his colleagues Adrian Zackheim, Nina Rodríguez-Marty, and Lillian Ball have been both consummate professionals and joys to work with.

Neil Gordon read every word of multiple versions of the manuscript and helped us in countless ways to make the ideas easy to understand.

: ACKNOWLEDGMENTS

Very early in the process Mark Levy helped us to figure out what the most important ideas were and how to articulate them. Doug Eymer worked with us to create visual elements to tell the story. Stacy Willis and Ashleigh Respicio helped us build out our website, while David Jackel and Shana Bethune worked with us on video. Nathan Gray, Lider Sucre, Colin Wiel, and T. J. Kanczuzewski from Geoversity provided support from the jungle's edge.

Boston's GrubStreet writing community has been invaluably supportive of the careers of both David and Reiko. We are never far from inspiration in the form of classes and the friends we've made there.

Perhaps most important, Yukari Watanabe Scott, wife and mother to us, listened, provided valuable counsel, and knew when to let us make mistakes.

David:

First, a disclosure: Because I do advisory work, run seminars, and do paid speaking gigs based on the concepts of fanocracy, there are inevitable conflicts. Some of the people I write about in these pages are my friends, and I have run seminars for or advised several of the companies mentioned in the book.

A particular thank-you goes to Tony D'Amelio, who manages my speaking activities. Tony provided much valuable advice for this book as I was struggling to articulate the stories I wanted to tell from the stage. Tony and his colleagues Mirjana Novkovic, Matt Anderson, Carin Kalt, Meg Joray, and Jenny Taylor play critically important roles in making sure that my ideas are delivered effectively to audiences around the world.

I am grateful to Tony Robbins for bringing me into the Business Mastery community, where I present several times a year and deliver my New Marketing Mastery program. Thank you, Tony, for your wonderful foreword to *Fanocracy*, and thank you to the entire team at Robbins Research International, especially Diane Adcock.

Other people who have influenced me and whose thoughts are represented in these pages include Seth Godin, Bob Lefsetz, Vin Gaeta, Phillip Stutts, Anthony Venus, Dharmesh Shah, Scott Harris, Carolyn Kim, Rebecca Keat, Mitch Jackson, Verne Harnish, John Harris, and Jeff Ernst.

I met our wonderful photographer, Bruce Rogovin, at a Bob Weir & RatDog concert fifteen years ago, and he has shot all my portraits since then! Fanocracy at work!

The ideas in this book would never have emerged in my mind without my friends who share the same fandoms as me. Fellow Apollo lunar program aficionados include Larry, Rich, Jason, Chris, Leslie, and Steve. *"We are JAFSC!"* As of this writing, I've been to over 780 concerts since I was a teenager in the 1970s. I've most enjoyed going to shows with a crew of friends, and those live music enthusiasts over the years have helped shape my life and career. Thank you especially to Brian, Joe B., Meredith, Gavin, Jennie, Berkeley, Bill, Rick, Jay, Alan, Peter, and, of course, Reiko, who are always up for a show. *"These are the Good Old Days."* —Bh

Reiko:

The first to hear about these ideas, before they were ever meant to be in a book, were my friends who have been having discussions about fandom for years. Hannah, who encouraged my very first foray into fan fiction and feminist theory, and Victoria, who still helps me on every story. Jenny and Claire, my Morrigans and fellow Lions, will always be down for an all-too-serious talk about not-so-serious topics. Anna, who has traveled with me through real and fantastical lands, and who is always eager to talk about a good book. Nina, who is also making a career of her brilliant insight into pop culture, and who made watching terrible live-action anime remakes an anthropological adventure.

I also have to thank all the friends who have gotten me through school so far on TV and snacks. My Columbia crew, Sophia, Marina, Amy, Katja (*Sherlock*, *Doctor Who*, BBC specials, and Flamin' Hot Cheetos). The egg chat (Terrace House and "coward" omurice). Anthony (Asian cooking YouTube channels and every comfort food known to man) and the Glitters**ts (Sketchy, anime, and leftover lunch talk pizza).

And, of course, Ben, whose passion in everything he does is a bigger inspiration to me than he knows.

We would love to hear from you, especially if you'd like to share a fanocracy you are passionate about or one that you've created!

—David Meerman Scott (@dmscott) and Reiko Scott (@allison_reiko),
www.fanocracy.com

INDEX

ABOUT THE AUTHORS

David Meerman Scott:

David Meerman Scott straddles the baby boomer generation and Generation X. He's the same age as the *Brady Bunch* kids and grew up when everybody watched the same television shows—*The Partridge Family, Little House on the Prairie,* and *Happy Days*—and discussed them at school the next day. Today, he has three major fandoms. His collection of artifacts from the Apollo lunar program is said to be one of the best in the world, and he showcases this passion in a home museum and at ApolloArtifacts.com and ApolloPressKits.com. He loves surfing and enjoys getting into the waves when he is traveling the world delivering speeches. He has surfed Australia, Indonesia, Thailand, Puerto Rico, Costa Rica, Hawaii, and multiple spots on both coasts of the continental United States. He is also a massive live music fan and to date has seen over 780 live shows.

Early in his career he worked in New York, Tokyo, and Hong Kong in the global financial information business. Now living in Boston, he serves as an adviser to select emerging companies that are working to transform their industries by creating disruptive products and services, and he delivers speeches at events and runs seminars for companies around the world. To date David has presented in forty-six countries and on all seven continents.

A graduate of Kenyon College, David lives in the suburbs of Boston.

Check out his blog at DavidMeermanScott.com, and follow him on Twitter @dmscott.

Fanocracy is his eleventh book.

Reiko Scott:

At age twenty-six, Reiko is a mixed-race millennial who is just a few years older than members of Generation Z. The first Harry Potter book came out when she was five years old, the first Lord of the Rings movie when she was eight, and the first iPhone when she was thirteen. She's participated in the growth of online fandom through its many iterations, from LiveJournal to Tumblr to Discord, and has watched as her generation interweaves social justice more and more with entertainment. She graduated from Columbia University in the City of New York with a degree in neuroscience and is currently a student at Boston University School of Medicine.

Reiko is also an avid writer of speculative fiction. She graduated from the 2017 VONA/Voices writing workshop for people of color, and her short story "Phantom Limb" was published in Book Smugglers Publishing's *Awakenings* anthology in 2018. She has written fan fiction and drawn fan art for stories from books like Harry Potter to video games like *Mass Effect* to TV shows like *Avatar: The Last Airbender*.

Fanocracy is her first book.